With the Nation Watching

With the Nation Watching

Watching

Report of the Twentieth Century Fund Task Force on Televised Presidential Debates

---

Background Paper
by Lee M. Mitchell

LEXINGTON BOOKS
D. C. Heath and Company
Lexington, Massachusetts
Toronto

Library of Congress Cataloging in Publication Data

Main entry under title:

With the nation watching.

Includes bibliographical references.
CONTENTS: Report of the Twentieth Century Fund Task Force on Tele-
vised Presidential Debates.—Mitchell, L. M. Background paper.
1. Television in politics—United States. 2. Campaign debates—United
States. 3. Presidents—United States—Election. I. Mitchell, Lee M. Back-
ground paper for The Twentieth Century Fund Task Force on Televised Presi-
dential Debates. 1979. II. Twentieth Century Fund. Task Force on Televised
Presidential Debates. Report of the Twentieth Century Fund Task Force on
Televised Presidential Debates. 1979.
HE8700.7.P6W63   329'.01   79-14492
ISBN 0-87078-149-9
ISBN 0-87078-148-0 pbk.

Printed in the United States of America.

Paperbound International Standard Book Number: 0-87078-148-0

Clothbound International Standard Book Number: 0-87078-149-9

Library of Congress Catalog Card Number: 79-14492

179259

CONTENTS

FOREWORD

Memory plays tricks, but most Americans old enough to have watched Richard M. Nixon and John F. Kennedy stage their series of televised "debates" in 1960 retain indelible impressions of the event. The success of the debates, in particular the huge audiences they attracted, made it seem at the time that joint appearances on television of the leading contenders for the nation's highest office would become a permanent fixture in presidential campaigns. But sixteen years passed before another series of debates took place, this time featuring Jimmy Carter and Gerald Ford, the incumbent, although one not elected to the office, who proved willing to debate because he was trailing in public opinion polls. Again, huge audiences watched the two side by side on their television screens. Yet the debates, because of regulatory restraints and political maneuvering, have not become an integral part of the process of electing the president.

Because 1980 is only the second time the opportunity to mount debates in two consecutive campaigns has presented itself, the Trustees of the Twentieth Century Fund decided to establish an independent Task Force to consider whether debates are of value to the public and, if they are, how the major candidates could be encouraged to agree to joint appearances. This venture was part of the Fund's continuing program of research on communications and politics that produced *Voters' Time*, the report of the Fund's independent Commission on Campaign Costs in the Electronic Era, *Presidential Television* by Newton N. Minow, John Bartlow Martin, and Lee M. Mitchell, and *Openly Arrived At: Report of the Twentieth Century Fund Task Force on Broadcasting and the Legislature*. Hence, examining the feasibility of televised presidential debates, and doing so well before the next presiden-

tial campaign and the hurly-burly that will attend it, was a logical next
step in the Fund's work in the area.

The Fund's interest in such research was known to other institutions, some of which had been involved in one way or another with
previous debates; therefore, when planning the establishment of the
Task Force, the Fund decided to invite the Benton Foundation, the
John and Mary R. Markle Foundation, and the William and Flora Hew-
lett Foundation to act as co-sponsors. They all did so. In addition, the
Aspen Institute, whose intervention in the form of the so-called *Aspen*
ruling had helped to make possible the 1976 debates, cooperated on the
project. Thus, the Task Force was supported by a group of sponsors
diverse in their origins, interests, and geography.

This diversity was also present on the Task Force itself, a group of
distinguished Americans, all of whom were experienced one way or
another in broadcasting, journalism, and public affairs. The Task
Force did not begin its deliberations with a single mind about either the
value of debates or ways and means of assuring their continuation. On
the contrary, it engaged in long and spirited debate over their usefulness, expressing considerable concern over their emphasis on image
and on slips of the tongue, which made them seem to some participants
the "Superbowl" of politics. There also was criticism of the rigid formats used in the earlier debates, which had raised questions about
whether the debates were as spontaneous and as informative as they
ought to be. Yet after further consideration, the Task Force reached
the unanimous conclusion that presidential debates should be a customary event in presidential campaigns, although not by fiat.

Once that decision was made, the Task Force went on to the knotty
problems of how the debates should be organized and produced. Before arriving at its recommendations, it viewed excerpts from previous
debates and heard from a variety of guest witnesses involved in their
arrangements, production, and staging. The Task Force, the Fund, and
its co-sponsors are grateful to all those who made presentations and
entered into discussions with the Task Force: Robert Squire, The
Communications Company, Washington, D.C.; Steven Simmons, Domestic Policy Staff, The White House; Myles Martel, School of Arts
and Letters, West Chester State College; Henry Geller, Assistant
Secretary for Communications and Information, National Telecom-
munications and Information Administration; Chloe W. Aaron, Senior
Vice-President, Public Broadcasting Service; Frank Stanton, former
President, CBS; Ruth Hinerfeld and Elizabeth Dribben, the League of
Women Voters; Michael Raoul-Duval, President, Industrial Products
Group, the Mead Corporation; Jim Karayn, President, WHYY, Inc.;
F. Clifton White, F. Clifton White Associates, Inc.; Barry Jagoda, The
White House; Newton N. Minow, Sidley & Austin; William Rusher,

National Review; John Armor, Baltimore, Maryland; Lester Crystal, President, NBC News; Richard Wald, Senior Vice-President, ABC News; Sander Vanocur, ABC News Bureau; Charls E. Walker, Washington, D.C.; Richard Salant, CBS News.

Their contribution was most helpful, although the Task Force assumes full responsibility for its own recommendations.

The Task Force also benefited from the assistance of Lee M. Mitchell, who wrote the factual background paper on debates and the presidential election process that accompanies the report and served as Task Force rapporteur. Lee Mitchell's knowledge of the subject, particularly his authoritative grasp of communications law and regulation, proved an invaluable resource, as it had been in his previous work for the Fund.

All of the sponsors owe a special debt to the Task Force itself. It is really unfair to single out individual members of the Task Force because all were devoted and conscientious participants in its discussions and decisions. Yet I must make mention of Douglass Cater, its able chairman, who exhibited sure instincts in knowing when to permit his colleagues to engage in freewheeling debate and when to goad them into concentrating on specific issues, and of William Small, who proved the lone dissenter on one critical issue—the issue of sponsorship of the debates—and dissented in so principled and gentlemanly a fashion that he won increased respect from the majority. To both of them, and to all the members of the Task Force, we owe our thanks.

The Report of the Task Force does not assure that there will be debates in 1980 and beyond. But its observations on the importance of making use of television and its recommendations for exploiting its potential should stimulate both attention and action. In essence, the Report offers a thoughtful blueprint designed to make the debates more attractive to the candidates and more interesting and informative to the voting public. Whether or not its plans are followed in every particular, it will succeed if it arouses political and public interest in seeing to it that debates are held.

M. J. Rossant, DIRECTOR
THE TWENTIETH CENTURY FUND
APRIL 1979

Task Force Members

Douglass Cater, chairman,
president, Observer International, Inc.,
Washington, D.C.

Douglas L. Bailey,
president, Bailey, Deardourff &
Associates, Inc.

James David Barber,
professor of political science,
Duke University

Elizabeth S. Carpenter,
consultant, The Friends of the Lyndon
Baines Johnson Library

William H. Donaldson,
dean, School of Organization and
Management, Yale University

Philip L. Geyelin,
editorial page editor,
Washington Post

Richard Hatcher,
mayor, Gary, Indiana

Norman Lear,
television producer,
Los Angeles

Roland Nachman,
attorney,
Montgomery, Alabama

John O. Pastore,
formerly Senator from Rhode Island;
chairman of the board, Columbus
National Bank, Providence

Gene Pokorny,
executive vice-president, Cambridge
Reports, *Cambridge, Massachusetts*

Herbert Schmertz,
vice-president, public affairs,
Mobil Oil Corporation

William Small,
vice-president, CBS Inc.

Percy Sutton,
formerly Manhattan Borough President;
attorney, Phillips, Nizer, Benjamin,
Krim and Ballon

Helen Thomas,
White House correspondent,
UPI

Lee M. Mitchell, rapporteur,
attorney, Sidley & Austin

Report of the Task Force

The American citizenry, according to all of the available evidence, shows discontent and distrust toward politicians and political parties. Despite the extension of the franchise to younger age groups and previously disenfranchised minorities, there has been continuing decline in voter turnout in both national and local elections. Clearly, Americans have not been engaged by politics in the way that they were in the not-so-distant past.

This Task Force regards the disappointing trend in voter turnout as a challenge, not a cause for despair. We are dedicated to the proposition that citizens should go to the polls of their own volition and that a free citizenry, capable of making an informed choice, is the best assurance of responsive, democratic government.

Our deliberations, which have focused on the election of the nation's chief executive, have identified many shortcomings in the political process, some of which may not be easily amenable to change. In this Report, however, we deal solely with the role of television debates in political campaigning, and in particular with their importance in presidential elections. The Task Force has found two major problems that call for constructive action.

First, there has been a revolutionary change in the ways in which we engage in political communication. Television has become the primary campaign medium. Yet, while television allows the candidates to reach more people than ever before, and to do so in the intimacy of their homes where they can see and hear, compare and judge candidates for leadership, it has not served to bring greater public interest in the elections or to give the public a clearer picture of the differences among candidates. The great promise of television as a means of informing—and involving—potential voters has not yet been fulfilled.

Second, federal law and regulations on broadcast practices have restricted robust political debate on television during the formal election campaign, which is precisely the time it could be most beneficial. The requirement of Section 315 of the Communications Act that *all* candidates for the presidency have "equal time" on a broadcast station if any candidate appears on the station has served to reduce the opportunity of the public to see and hear the most significant candidates.[1]

This Task Force has examined the two notable instances in which an effort was made to meet these problems—the televised presidential debates of 1960 and 1976. In 1960, Congress temporarily suspended Section 315 to permit the events to be broadcast by the television networks free of the "equal time" burden; John Kennedy and Richard Nixon were willing to confront each other in presidential debates. In 1976, a Federal Communications Commission (FCC) decision, known as the *Aspen* ruling, enabled the networks to broadcast the events under the sponsorship and control of the nonprofit, nonpartisan League of Women Voters without incurring "equal time" obligations;[2] Jimmy Carter and Gerald Ford (as well as their vice-presidential nominees) agreed to engage in joint appearances.

These two exceptions, sixteen years apart, established precedent without providing guarantees for the future. The mission of this Task Force has been to make recommendations about presidential debates for 1980 and beyond. In carrying out our assignment, we have endeavored to weigh the citizen interest as compared with the particular interests of the candidates, the media, and other parties. Our purpose has been to consider how well these debates can help provide insight into the leadership potential of the contestants, and thereby help promote informed judgments by the nation's voters.

We are keenly aware that presidential debates cannot and should not be conducted in a vacuum: they must be part of the larger political process by which the American public is exposed to ideas, issues, and candidates. Still, television with its ubiquitous presence has effectively transformed electoral politics. Opinion is divided about its impact, but whether it has been good or bad—and this Task Force believes that it has been both good and bad—it cannot be wished away. There have been many controversial aspects of television campaigning—the attempts to sell candidates through the repetition of advertising spots, the excessive emphasis on coverage of "image" rather than issues, the loss of a sense of personal contact between the candidate and the public. But we do not believe that the solution lies in further restrictions. On the contrary, this Task Force is convinced that there is an urgent need for more imaginative and appropriate uses of television in the political process and that doing so can serve to make it a more positive and useful medium. **We have confined our scope to the single task of determining how presidential debates, carried simultaneously over the airwaves and reported extensively by other media, can contribute to the informing and educating of the American public on the choice vital to the future of the nation.**

Value of the Presidential Debates

The joint appearances of 1960 and 1976, featured as the Presidential Debates, successfully attracted and sustained the attention of many more citizens than any other forums of the election year: primaries, party conventions, candidate TV and radio appearances, paid political commercials. For most citizens, they provided the only opportunity to observe the contenders in a common setting and in comparatively unrehearsed circumstances. There is limited evidence of their impact on the electorate. Whether and by how much they generated an increased turnout or actually changed voter preference cannot be measured with precision. Nevertheless, the Task Force believes that past debates were informative and that they stimulated voter interest.

Misgivings have been voiced by some critics that these presidential debates corrupted the political process. They argue:

• Too much attention was devoted to which contestant won or lost each bout, not how well each one clarified his position on the issues.

• The slip of the tongue tended to get more publicity than the gravity of the arguments.

• Debating skill has nothing to do with the awesome requirements for leading a nation.

• Image is emphasized at the expense of substance.

We note these anxieties without succumbing to them. Whatever their weaknesses, the debates were the only time during two presidential campaigns that the two major candidates appeared together side by side and under conditions that they did not control. The debates also exposed partisan supporters of each candidate to the views and personality of his opponent. And they served to generate heightened public interest and controversy over the candidates and the issues.

Moreover, an overwhelming number of those who followed the debates reached the conclusion that they were worthwhile endeavors in the public interest. Both candidates in 1976 attested afterward to their value. Among the many events of the campaign, these joint appearances constituted rare occasions when, as one broadcast leader noted following the 1960 debates, citizens could observe and judge the major candidates together "in the act of being alive."[3] How well a candidate survives this test, which goes far beyond the skillful use of language, provides one significant measure of capacity for leadership.

This Task Force has concluded that presidential debates should become a regular and customary feature of the presidential election campaign, not an occasional and fortuitous event that takes place many years apart. **At the same time, the Task Force rejects the suggestion that the debates should be made mandatory for the candidates, by either law or regulation. We favor creating conditions which will encourage candidates to participate and broadcasters to provide coverage.** The following recommendations represent our judgment about those conditions which will best serve the public interest in these debates.

Sponsorship

The two series of presidential debates we have witnessed to date had different forms of sponsorship. In 1960, the debates were sponsored and produced by the broadcast networks, acting in concert after negotiations with representatives of the major party nominees. In 1976, under the terms of the FCC's *Aspen* ruling, the League of Women Voters served as sponsor while the broadcasters were permitted to cover the debates as bona fide news events.

After lengthy deliberation, involving consultation with a number of expert witnesses and consideration of many options, **a substantial majority of the Task Force concluded that sponsorship for the debates should follow the 1976 precedent—that a nonprofit, nonpartisan citizen group devoted to citizen education and participation should act as the sponsor. For the 1980 campaign, we therefore recommend that the League of Women Voters continue as sponsor.** In our view, the League is well qualified for this responsibility because of its long history of voter education and the experience it gained from its role in the 1976 debates. If the League decides against acting as sponsor, we urge that other nonprofit, nonpartisan groups and associations, free of governmental or corporate ties, take on this responsibility. After 1980, we believe that further thought should be given to assembling a broad consortium of nonpartisan citizens' groups to serve as regular sponsor.

In carrying out the objectives set forth in this Report, **the Task Force recommends that the League—or other sponsoring nonprofit, nonpartisan groups—establish a Presidential Debates Committee to advise it on all matters pertaining to the debates,** such as which candidates should be invited to participate, what formats should be used, and the choice of the interrogators who will pose questions.

The members of the proposed Presidential Debates Committee should be distinguished citizens representative of the major elements in our society—business, labor, education, religion, the press, the arts, racial and ethnic minorities, and political organizations. In addition, and to the extent that legal regulations allow, the major broadcast networks should have representation. Although the League or other sponsor would retain organizational control of the presidential debates, the proposed advisory Committee would provide a degree of public participation in planning the debates and bring to bear on difficult decisions a broad range of informed opinion.

We believe it essential that the Presidential Debates Committee be formed early in the election year or, preferably, in the preceding year, and that the League present a fully formed debate proposal in advance of the party conventions. With the assistance of this Committee, the League should make the candidates aware at an early date of the form in which it believes the debates would best serve the public, rather than wait for the candidates to specify the conditions under which they would consider participating.

Both the proceedings for planning the debates and the negotiations with candidate representatives should be made public. **The public has a right to know what conditions, if any, have been stipulated by candidates, while the candidates should be aware that they cannot take a private position in dealing with the sponsor and a different position with the public.**

We believe that debates organized in this manner can be broadcast by the television networks without "equal time" obligations in the spirit of the *Aspen* ruling. Based on their past performance, we believe the networks will broadcast these events with the same professionalism they have applied to other important national events. We urge, however, that the FCC clarify the *Aspen* ruling to eliminate any doubt that the networks may cooperate closely with the League in making arrangements for television coverage of the debates.

The Task Force recognizes that the broadcast networks will seek to take responsibility for organizing the debates if Congress permits them to. All but one member of the Task Force voiced strong reservations about whether the networks, which will be simultaneously broadcasting the debates, provide the proper auspices for organizing them. Such a joint sponsorship might exercise undue influence over the electoral process. Critical choices will have to be made in the course of negotiating the debates—particularly on whether to include "significant" third candidates—which require decisions that have unassailable public credibility. We do not believe such decisions can be based simply on news judgment, which is the guide for the networks and other news-gathering organizations. An organization committed to voter education and representing wide citizen involvement can provide more appropriate sponsorship.*

At the same time, we favor providing broadcasters the freedom to present more programming and a greater variety of programming devoted to the presidential contest. The Task Force supports efforts in Congress to modify Section 315 of the Communications Act in order to remove restrictions on broadcast coverage of the presidential election

---

William Small dissents:

As the only veteran of broadcast journalism on the Task Force, I feel compelled to dissent, not because I am opposed to the League of Women Voters sponsoring debates, but because I am opposed to the specific exclusion of broadcasters from such sponsorship.

I have spent over a quarter of a century fighting governmental intrusion into broadcast journalism because I feel that the provisions of the First Amendment cover radio and television as well as the printed press. In my view, the fairness doctrine and Section 315 violate both the spirit and the language of the free speech and free press provisions of the First Amendment. Sadly, there are those in Congress, the regulatory agencies, and the judiciary who do not agree.

Broadcasters and newspapers *have* "sponsored" candidate debates on the local and state levels for many years. I know of no incident where their sponsorship created moral or ethical problems or lacked "public credibility"—before or after the event. The same can be said safely of the network arrangements of the 1960 presidential debates. (Continued on page 8)

process to permit this greater freedom.[4] **But the special role that presidential debates can play in the electoral process calls for their sponsorship by a nonprofit, nonpartisan organization.** If and when there is a modification of Section 315, we urge Congress to make clear through legislative language that the presidential debates should have such a nonbroadcast sponsor. This expression of congressional intent will be particularly urgent if the modification takes place after the beginning of 1980, when plans for the debates may be well under way and when modification could cause confusion concerning the respective roles of the networks and the League in organization of the debates.

Participation of Major Party Nominees

In 1976, Gerald Ford set the precedent of participation by an incumbent president. Later, he urged that the debates should be continued in future presidential elections. Both Ford and Carter acknowledged that the debates played an important and useful role in their contest. Nevertheless, the absence of debates during all but two presidential elections has been due to the reluctance of the major party nominees, the incumbent in particular, to take part in these encounters.

We are willing to accept the decision of a candidate to decline to participate and to let the voter determine what weight to give to that decision. The Task Force does not believe that a candidate for the nation's highest office should be told how to conduct an effective, informative campaign. Taking this discretion away from the candidates would be to eliminate one basis for making judgments about them.

The Task Force, however, takes the position that presidential candidates—including an incumbent president—have an obligation to the electorate to face each other in televised debates. If the League of Women Voters or a similar highly regarded nonprofit, nonpartisan organization sponsors debates in future years, establishes an advisory Committee of leading citizens, and presents the candidates with a carefully planned debate proposal, any candidate who refuses to participate must bear the burden of explaining and justifying such a decision.

(Continued from page 7)

Moreover, a full lifting of Section 315 does not preclude sponsorship by the League and others; in fact, in 1976 it would have permitted the networks to provide studios or to have contributed to the cost of renting the debate sites and prevented the League from incurring its large debt.

I am sorry that my colleagues on the Task Force, diligent and thoughtful as they have been, have shown a lack of faith in such network participation. I do not believe the public at large shares their conclusion.

I want to make clear that I admire the League generally and its hard work in producing the 1976 debates particularly. In fact, over twenty years ago, I produced and moderated televised debates in Kentucky with the League as co-sponsor and participant.

I just feel it improper to exclude broadcasters.

Participation of Other Candidates

Accommodating major candidates who are not representatives of the nation's two major parties presents the single most difficult issue confronting presidential debates. Historically, the United States has been served by a two-party system, but not the two parties presently playing the dominant roles. Third-party challengers have on occasion shaped the course of our politics. Even though only the candidates of the two major parties appeared in the previous presidential debates, this Task Force believes that if "significant" third-party candidates emerge, they should be invited to participate in future presidential debates. The problem is to recognize the claim of significant contenders while not giving added encouragement to the splinter or marginal or single-issue candidates who proliferate in presidential election years.

The Task Force has examined many precedents for determining what qualifications make a "significant" candidate: requirements for federal campaign funding, Secret Service criteria for providing candidate protection, FCC "Equal Time" and "Reasonable Access" rulings, as well as the *Voters' Time* recommendation of an earlier Twentieth Century Fund Commission. None, in our opinion, provides an adequate or foolproof formula. We have concluded that criteria for selecting such participants cannot be fixed in advance. This difficulty increases the responsibility placed on the debate sponsor to make recommendations that will be publicly recognized as equitable.

We recommend that, as in other Western democracies, a rule of reason should guide the sponsor in determining who should participate in the debate series. The standards should be high. Our intent is not to eliminate vigorous competition for the presidency, but to restrict the number who share platform time in nationally simulcast presidential debates. In particular we favor the claim of a significant third-party nominee over that of a candidate who pursues a loner's course.*

We suggest that the sponsor and Presidential Debate Committee should set a minimum requirement ensuring that a candidate must qualify to appear on the ballot in a sufficient number of states to constitute an electoral college majority. In addition, the candidate might be required to meet one or more of the following:

• Be the nominee of a party which received at least 5 percent of the popular vote in the previous election;

Douglass Cater comments:
   I am concerned that the debates not encourage any candidate's strategy to throw the presidential election into the House of Representatives where, by the Constitution's provision that each state's delegation shall cast a single vote, the contest would be resolved by a highly divisive as well as undemocratic process.

• Have been nominated by a party primary or state convention in a majority of states;

• Have obtained signed petitions from 15 percent of the voters in a majority of states;

• Be able to provide evidence of significant popular support in the major polls;

• Be supported by a national political organization with other candidates or elected public officials.

No law or regulation can compel major candidates to confront third-party or independent contenders. It would be ridiculous if, in an effort to include others, the Presidential Debate Committee should succeed in eliminating participation of the major party nominees. If the major party nominees make known their refusal to participate with a candidate or candidates determined by the sponsor to be significant minority or independent candidates, the sponsor should organize and attempt to obtain broadcast coverage of alternative forums for the minority candidates.[5] The argument has been made that any alternatives will result in smaller audiences for the minor candidates. But this condition existed well before the era of broadcasting.

Format

While specific arrangements will be negotiated by the sponsor and the Presidential Debate Committee, we suggest that four presidential—and one vice-presidential—debates are an adequate number spaced over the formal campaign period. We urge avoidance of the overly rigid formats of the previous debates; instead, they should be varied on different occasions to allow greater flexibility and more opportunity for the contestants to shape the substance of the debates. Among our suggestions:

• **During the opening session, each candidate should be permitted substantial time to spell out his major positions, at length and without interruptions.** These statements, with brief rejoinders, would constitute the substance that would be developed in subsequent debates.

• **While recognizing the reluctance of the candidates in 1960 and 1976 to address each other directly, we do not believe that interrogators should play the principal role in setting the debate agenda.** A more appropriate format would allow interrogation by others, but retain time for the candidates to address arguments and questions to one another.

• **The Presidential Debates Committee should prepare a roster that in-**

cludes not only journalists and commentators but the other representatives of our society from which balanced panels of interrogators would be selected.

• For at least one debate, each candidate might designate two or three associates to pose questions and assist in responding to questions in an adversary proceeding.

• Within the time limits of each debate—90 minutes being reasonable—the candidate should be allowed some freedom in controlling his total allotment rather than being confined to rigid time restraints for each response and counterresponse.

• **The final debate of the series should be scheduled at least one week before election day** in order to discourage last-minute allegations which cannot be immediately answered. It should permit substantial time for each candidate to sum up his position in a manner of his own choosing.

• Taking note of the dispute in 1976 over whether broadcasters should be permitted "reaction shots" of the audience, **we recommend, subject to legal requirements, against an immediate audience that might by its behavior inject its own partisan feelings into the proceedings.**

• Rather than limiting postmortem judgment following each debate to the press and a few prominent critics, we recommend encouraging community response throughout the nation. Public broadcasting stations, for example, could hold televised forums which would involve a cross-section of the citizenry for the purpose of analyzing and arguing about what it has just witnessed. Commercial stations should devise similar opportunities for televised local discussion of the debates.

In brief, while not clinging to the classic debate format, we believe strongly that the format should encourage more initiative by the candidates, more direct confrontation and rejoinders, and more opportunity for each candidate to determine the length and thrust of his arguments.

Financing

We welcome offers by the broadcasters to provide without charge adequate prime air time to meet reasonable schedules for the debates. We recommend that in 1980 direct costs for staging the presidential debates should be raised by contributions to the League of Women Voters Education Fund. **We urge the Federal Election Commission to issue—and Congress to sustain—a ruling to permit solicitation of funding from corporate, labor union, and foundation sources, well in advance of the election year.**

Expanding the Public Forum of the Presidential Election Contest

Throughout our deliberations, we have recognized that presidential debates make only one contribution to the larger "forum of democracy" represented by the campaign. Choosing a president is too important to be relegated to any one form of contest. We recommend:

• **Broadcasters should be encouraged to develop a greater variety of programs to inform the citizenry about the presidency, the candidates, and the political process.** The challenge goes well beyond election year coverage. It must include more interviews to identify potential candidates, not simply the self-declared aspirants; more documentaries devoted to basic issues as well as to candidates; more forums in which citizens get a chance to have their say; more programs devoted to problems of the presidency itself.

• **Revision of Section 315 of the Communications Act, with congressional stipulation that presidential debates should have nonpartisan, nonprofit sponsorship, can offer broadcasters new encouragement to create this larger forum of democracy.** At the same time, we urge all broadcasters—and the print press as well—to adopt and publicize voluntary standards to assure accuracy and fairness in the treatment of presidential candidates, including opportunity for timely corrections and rebuttals. We endorse the proposal by broadcast executives that free time be made available to candidates for use as they judge best.

Conclusion

Voter apathy and dissatisfaction undoubtedly stem from varied causes. The issues confronting this nation appear to become increasingly complicated and not susceptible to quick and easy solution. Professional pressure groups have grown in power and pervasiveness. Political parties no longer command the passionate partisanship they once did. Even efforts at reforms have had the side effect of contributing to a decline in direct citizen participation in the political campaigns mounted by the parties. Instead of party-based coalitions, we are seeing personality-based campaigns, which may attract the support of some citizens but repel many others. Under such circumstances, the citizen has increased difficulty convincing himself that his vote can make a difference in the course of events.

Yet the nation is clearly committed to democratic government, and this Task Force has faith in the basic strength and good sense of the American body politic. What is needed is wit and imagination and the will to make the political process work more effectively. We are convinced that these qualities are what can make political television realize its enormous potential for informing and enriching the electorate.

The presentation of presidential debates every four years as a regular feature of presidential election campaigns would be a useful start to a new and more exciting exposure of the candidates via television.

If the debates for 1980 are to become a reality, they cannot be left to chance. They must be planned for. The time to start is now.

NOTES

1. Section 315 requires that, if a broadcast station makes time available to one candidate for the presidency (or for any other elective office), it must make "equal opportunities" available to all other candidates for that office. This requirement is often called the "equal time" provision and is interpreted and enforced by the Federal Communications Commission (FCC).

2. Section 315 exempts from the "equal time" requirement appearances by candidates in certain types of television programming, including "on-the-spot coverage of bona fide news events." In response to a petition filed by the Aspen Institute, the FCC ruled in 1975 that broadcast of debates between candidates could be considered "on-the-spot coverage of bona fide news events" so long as the debates were organized by a group not affiliated with the broadcaster, carried live in their entirety, and not intended to give a political advantage to a particular candidate. This interpretation was upheld by the federal courts.

3. Frank Stanton, former president of CBS.

4. The Task Force favors the retention of what is known as the FCC's "fairness doctrine," which, in the context of a presidential election, requires that a broadcaster make a reasonable judgment in good faith as to the significance of the competing candidates and, in light of their respective significance, how much coverage should be provided their candidacies. The Task Force also favors retention of the statutory requirement that broadcasters provide "reasonable access" to their facilities for candidates in the form of either free or purchased spot and program time.

5. Without a modification of Section 315, appearances of the minority candidates other than in a debate might be subject to the "equal time" requirement, which would impede broadcast coverage.

Additional Comments

by Norman Lear

I am proud of the work that has been completed by the Task Force on Presidential Television Debates. However, I want to add an addendum to paragraph two of the section. "Expanding the Public Forum of the Presidential Election Contest," wherein we recognize that "Broadcasters should be encouraged to develop a greater variety of programs to inform the citizenry about the presidency, the candidates, and the political process. The challenge goes well beyond election year coverage." I believe that it is leadership's responsibility—and we, the Task Force on Presidential Television Debates, comprise in part that "leadership"—to illuminate issues for the electorate and that we should go far beyond encouraging broadcasters to develop programs which might do so.

I believe it is possible to develop a format for discussions of public issues that could—and should—lead to their being aired on national television three or four times a year, leading every fourth year to the major event, the presidential debates. We have a public hungry for information and understanding, which are currently lacking only because we have not provided the vehicles through which such information and understanding might be realized. The average family, with two or more children, living on a modest income, has all it can do to get from Monday to Friday. Leadership owes them more than the dry, passionless presentation of such public affairs programs as "Meet the Press," "Issues and Answers," etc. This electorate requires more showmanship and more passion in the presentation of issue-oriented programming if we are to hold its attention.

I believe that a format can be developed for the discussion of important issues wherein partisans on both sides meet each other head-on, moderated by an individual whose sole purpose is to steer the debate, allowing no participant to avoid a question or a challenge. For example, the sides are clearly drawn on the question of armaments and our

15

military budget. We all know those who believe our national security is threatened by the Soviet Union because we are falling seriously behind in the arms race; so, too, do we know the experts who believe we are *not* falling behind and that the facts and figures constantly provided by the other side are totally fallacious and are being propagated solely to keep us in a climate of fear for the benefit and profit of the military-industrial complex.

Given a proper format—for example, six passionate partisans, three on each side—this issue could be argued in the kind of freewheeling, hard-hitting discussion in which personalities get ruffled, skins get pricked, and passions flow. Such a program will capture the attention of the viewer who, by watching with his interest engaged, gains a basic understanding of the issue. The primary function of the program would not be to provide the viewers with the information they need to make a decision on the issues we choose for debate, but rather to get large numbers of viewers interested enough in those subjects to wish to learn even more about them so that they debate them in their own lives. That way, the debates will truly *involve* the audience, simultaneously appealing to its intellect and emotions. The scheduling of such discussions on a regular basis could attract a level of television ratings that the kind of issue-oriented programs mentioned above never receive. By virtue of such ratings, and by nature of the uninhibited, unrestrained discussion itself, we might be meeting what I see as our greatest responsibility.

We owe the American people a series of presidential debates every four years. But we owe them more. Programs on vital issues can be delivered in such a way as to ensure a large audience and a better understanding of the subjects under discussion.

Background Paper

by Lee M. Mitchell

I/Introduction

They came by train, in horse-drawn wagons, and on foot to the town square in Ottawa, Illinois. More than 12,000 citizens wanted to be present at this, the first of the scheduled debates between the candidates for the Illinois Senate seat that was to be filled in the November 1858 election. The crowd gathered in the square was so large it took the candidates half an hour to reach the hastily erected speaker's platform. That meeting between Stephen A. Douglas and Abraham Lincoln marked the first time in American history that candidates for high political office had met in so widely publicized a debate during a campaign. "The two were to stand . . . together and argue," wrote Carl Sandburg, "with all Illinois watching, and the whole country listening."[1]

The whole country did not, of course, listen. The inventions that would have allowed it to do so were still at least a half century in the future. But if the nation could not listen, at least many of its citizens could read. And in 1858, the newspapers—the only form of political mass communications—were able, by using the recently developed art of shorthand reporting, to carry a transcript of the Lincoln-Douglas debate across the country. The debates did more than help decide the election; although Lincoln lost the Senate seat, he became a nationally known figure because of them. The exposure he gained made it feasible for him to become the Republican candidate for the presidency in 1860—and to defeat Douglas in that contest.

The Lincoln-Douglas debates made possible the joint scrutiny of candidates that might, on first glance, have been expected to develop earlier in our democratic system of government. A closer look at American political history, however, reveals why such a development took so long. The framers of the American Constitution did not provide for direct election of senators or the president. Senators were originally chosen by the state legislatures, and the president was selected by the electoral college—a small group of persons believed to be of

19

superior knowledge and judgment. As long as selection of these high public officials did not rest directly with the public, there was no reason to campaign among the public; George Washington disassociated himself almost entirely from the first presidential election, and succeeding presidential candidates generally campaigned discreetly, if at all. It was not until the presidential primary was adopted in the early 1900s that the practice of campaigning among the people, as we know it today, became widely accepted. Given this history, the 1858 debates may have been ahead of their time.[2]

In any event, it was another one hundred years before presidential candidates appeared jointly in anything even resembling a debate. Richard M. Nixon and John F. Kennedy made history in 1960 by being the first candidates for the office of president to engage in a joint, debate-type* appearance; the audience they faced was not composed of 12,000 hardy individuals who had traveled to hear them, but rather 100 million individuals who had turned a dial. The difference, of course, was radio and television, which have become the primary means for the communication of political issues and images.

Once the public and the candidates had witnessed this marriage of political debate and television, all concerned confidently predicted that some form of televised presidential debate soon would become an American electoral tradition. In his closing words, the moderator of the final Kennedy-Nixon debate noted that "surely [these programs] have set a new precedent. Perhaps they have established a new tradition." Historian Theodore H. White proclaimed the debates "a revolution in American presidential politics."[3] And newsman Walter Lippmann wrote:

> The TV debate was a bold innovation that is bound to be carried forward to future campaigns, and could not now be abandoned. From now on it will be impossible for any candidate . . . to avoid this kind of confrontation with his opponent.[5]

The New York Times reported that it was "the general opinion that the public will demand these joint appearances in all future Presidential campaigns."[6] Two years later, the immediate impact of the events long past, Richard Nixon predicted that "debates between the Presidential candidates on television are a fixture, and in all the elections in the future we are going to have debates between the candidates."[7]

---

* The Kennedy-Nixon "debates" were not debates in the traditional sense, but rather joint television appearances in which the candidates answered questions from a panel. They are, however, commonly referred to as debates, a practice that will be followed here when referring to all similar joint appearances by candidates for political office.[4]

Televised presidential debates, however, did not become an institution. Indeed, they did not reappear until 1976, but then, in the form of the Carter-Ford debates, they again gave rise to confident predictions of their becoming an institution in American elections. "The American people," reported *Saturday Review*, "have made up their mind that TV debates are going to be an integral part of future presidential campaigns."[8]

Today, the future of televised presidential debates remains uncertain. Although the 1976 debates seemed to be another step in establishing a tradition, they were in many ways the result of the coming together of events—a set of coincidences—that may not occur in the same way again. The future of such debates is uncertain because presidential candidates have not demonstrated a common desire to include televised debates in each presidential election campaign; the general public is not sufficiently organized to demand that the candidates make debates part of the electoral process; and the television broadcast industry is impeded by legal restrictions that make it difficult for it to institutionalize the debates. Moreover, even if the factors that have made television debates possible in the past were to be present again in a given presidential year, the absence of an existing mechanism for organizing or paying for the debates reduces the likelihood of their materializing.

If past experience with televised presidential debates had not revealed their usefulness to the electoral process, their uncertain future might be of little concern. But the debates have demonstrated their potentially important place in the process of choosing a president by bringing the candidates before the largest audiences ever assembled in a campaign; by giving those audiences the opportunity to see the presidential candidates in a format or situation not wholly within the candidates' control (a rare occurrence in a campaign), and by serving as a useful check on the candidates' own versions of their character and positions as presented in candidate-produced commercials or by other stagecraft. The debates also presented voters with a unique opportunity to compare two candidates side by side. Not only is this kind of comparison useful for evaluating candidates, but more importantly, it brings those persons predisposed to favor one candidate into unavoidable contact with the other candidate. As Frank Stanton of CBS wrote following the 1960 debates, "By their very nature they expose the audience that tuned in to hear one man, the one it favored, to the views of the other man, the one it thought it opposed."[9]

Viewers of televised debates probably learn more about the candidates' personalities and their positions on issues than they would without them. The debates seem to sharpen the differences between candidates and sometimes to raise issues that otherwise might not be addressed. Surveys in 1960 reported that more than two-thirds of those who saw the debates thought them a good way to learn about campaign issues, and a 1976 survey found that two-thirds of its respondents favored debates in 1980.[10]

Televised debates, however, are not without their critics, some of whom charge that they encourage a cult of personality at the expense of careful consideration of issues and policies. For example, critic Sander Vanocur writes that they "are corruptive of the political process by placing a premium on performance and personality."[11] We are warned that they could bring about a political system dominated by demagogic television performers chosen on the basis of their TV image. Other critics argue that televised debates threaten to dominate elections to the exclusion of direct candidate contact with the public or other desirable exposure of the candidates. Still other critics fear that an election might be decided by a single misstatement made before 100 million persons.

These and other criticisms of televised debates, while not easily brushed aside, do not seem to provide sufficient reason for the recurrence of debates to be left to chance. Television has become an important part of the political process, perhaps even the most important part. The way a candidate is perceived on television, and his or her ability to use television effectively, is now as valid a test of leadership as was the candidate's ability to deliver an effective speech in the town square. In fact, given television's ability to take an issue directly to the entire American electorate over the opposition of Congress and the press, the ability to use television effectively may be an even better test. The debates are potentially too helpful in selecting a chief executive to discard them because they may also be potentially harmful. If they are to be a continuing part of the political scene, debates must be structured to maximize their contribution and to minimize their risk.

If televised debates between candidates for the presidency are to be a feature of future presidential elections, many issues remain to be resolved. First, of course, is the question of who is to be responsible for the continuance of the debates—candidates, broadcast networks, educational and service organizations, or the government? Closely related to this question is the issue of who should pay for the debates, an issue that raises both practical and legal problems. Next, is the question of how the participation of candidates can best be assured. And closely related to that question is the issue of whether candidates of minor parties or candidates without any party should have a place in the debates. Finally, there are many questions about the most desirable format for future debates. Finding the right answers could make televised presidential debates an important and constructive part of American elections in years to come.

II/Origins and History

In 1824, Thomas Jefferson observed that "in a republican nation, whose citizens are to be led by reason and persuasion and not by force, the art of reasoning becomes of first importance."[1] Throughout the nineteenth century, elected leaders often engaged in formal debates on important political and social issues, and the most skilled debaters often became well-known national figures. Debating—a major activity in the Congress—was used to resolve important national concerns. In 1830, for example, Senators Daniel Webster and Robert Y. Hayne engaged in a closely followed debate on the nature of the union of the American states. In the 1850s, Webster, Henry Clay, and John C. Calhoun engaged in an important three-way debate concerning the Compromise of 1850, which admitted pro- and antislavery territories to the Union without establishing a national position on slavery.

The First Campaign Debate: Lincoln-Douglas

In 1858, Abraham Lincoln, "the first and only choice of the Republicans," and Stephen A. Douglas, the Democratic incumbent, were preparing to campaign for election to the Senate from Illinois. Lincoln, the lesser known of the two, dispatched a handwritten challenge to Douglas:

> Will it be agreeable to you to make an arrangement for you and myself to divide time, and address the same audiences during the present canvas?[2]

Douglas accepted this challenge to debate and, as the incumbent and the challenged party, was given the right to choose the number and the location of the debates. He determined that seven debates would be

23

held, one in each of the Illinois congressional districts in which the two had not yet spoken. The first debate took place in Ottawa on August 21, 1858, and the others followed at intervals ranging from two days to more than two weeks.

The Lincoln-Douglas debates have been accorded an important place in history, not only because they apparently were the first public debates between candidates for a major political office, but also because they constituted an important discussion of the question of slavery, then the dominant issue in the country. All but one of the debates were devoted primarily to slavery and to the case of *Dred Scott v. Sandford*, decided by the Supreme Court the preceding year. The Court had held slavery to be constitutional and had ruled that the provisions of the Constitution relating to personal rights and privileges did not apply to slaves or their descendants. Lincoln argued that slavery was morally wrong and contrary to the nation's best interests. In the final debate, in Alton, Illinois, Lincoln summarized the position he had taken throughout the debates:

> Has anything ever threatened the existence of this Union save and except this very institution of slavery? This is the real issue. This is the issue that will continue in the country when these poor tongues of Judge Douglas and myself shall be silent. It is the eternal struggle between these two principles—right and wrong—throughout the world.[3]

Audiences for the debates ranged from more than 12,000 to a low of 1,500, but many more read lengthy accounts in the newspapers, which treated the proceedings as a news event of great significance. The supporters of both candidates concluded that their candidate had bested the other. A pro-Lincoln newspaper commented that "the Ottawa debate gave great satisfaction to our side. Mr. Lincoln we thought had the better of the argument, and we all came away encouraged also." But attention did not always seem to be focused on the substance of the argument. The pro-Douglas *Chicago Times* carried the following headline:

THE CAMPAIGN
Douglas Among the People.
Joint Discussion at Ottawa!
Lincoln Breaks Down.
Enthusiasm of the People!
Lincoln's Heart Fails Him!
Lincoln's Legs Fail Him!
Lincoln's Tongue Fails Him!
Lincoln's Arms Fail Him!
Lincoln Fails All Over!
The People Refuse to Support Him!
The People Laugh at Him!
Douglas the Champion of the People![4]

Douglas won the senatorial election that year, but the seeds of his political downfall were sown in the debates. In the second debate, in Freeport, Illinois, Lincoln had asked Douglas:

> Can the people of a United States Territory, in any lawful way and against the wish of any citizen of the United States, exclude slavery from its limits, prior to the formation of a State Constitution?[5]

Douglas said that slavery could indeed be excluded from a territory if the people of that territory chose to do so, antagonizing the slave-dependent South, where his answer became known as the "Freeport heresy." That answer cost Douglas the southern vote in the 1860 presidential election, and the public recognition Lincoln gained through the debates won him many a vote.

The Lincoln-Douglas debates may have represented a high point for the practice of debating important political issues. In the latter half of the nineteenth century, there were apparently fewer debates, and fewer leaders became known for their debating skills. The debate did not pass from political life unlamented. For example, a Mississippi politician wrote in 1889:

> Forty years ago, constant practice had made our public speakers so skillful in debate that every question was made clear even to men otherwise uneducated. For the last twenty years this practical union between politicians and people has not existed. Only one party is allowed to speak, and the leaders of that party no longer debate, they simply declaim and denounce. . . . Upon this crude and windy diet, the once robust and sturdy political convictions of our people have dwindled into leanness and decay. . . . The evil of mischievous assertion is greatly lessened when free discussion is allowed, and error exposed and combated by the unsparing vigor of an opposing party.[6]

Origins of Broadcast Debates

At the same time that the apparent demise of public debate was being mourned by some, experiments were taking place that would lead to a new means of airing public issues—the invention and development of radio and television broadcasting. By 1900, the wireless was becoming a popular mania, and the air was filled with the transmission of coded messages. It did not take long for voices to start replacing code; indeed, by 1915, "the air was a chaos of crackling codes, voices, and music."[7] These developments did not go unnoticed by Congress, whose members soon began to express concern that their opponents could dominate this new medium of communication. "The broadcasting field holds untold potentialities in a political . . . way," a congressional committee concluded, and "there is nothing . . . to prevent a broadcasting station from permitting . . . one candidate . . . to employ its service and refusing to accord the same right to the opposing side.''[8]

Radio coverage of the 1924 party conventions and the broadcast of campaign speeches by Calvin Coolidge in the election campaign of that year resulted in congressional hearings on possible unfairness in the treatment of candidates by broadcasters. And these hearings brought the first suggestion that political debates should be broadcast. William Harkness, an executive of American Telephone and Telegraph Company, suggested to the congressional committee that holding radio debates between the candidates would be a means of ensuring that a single candidate would not monopolize the air.[9] There is no indication that Congress, the candidates, or the broadcasters took note of the suggestion.

In 1927, Congress passed the first legislation comprehensively regulating radio broadcasting. One provision of the Radio Act of 1927 became known as the "equal time" requirement, and has remained in the law ever since. In its present form (Section 315 of the Communications Act of 1934), the provision states that "if any licensee [of a television or radio station] shall permit any person who is a legally qualified candidate for any public office to use a broadcasting station, he shall afford equal opportunities to all other such candidates for that office in the use of such broadcasting station."[10] The requirement—if a station allows one candidate to be seen or heard on its facilities, it must then allow all other candidates for the same office "equal opportunities" to be seen or heard—has proven to be one of the most controversial aspects of government regulation of the broadcast media and one of the largest stumbling blocks to conducting televised political debates.

Because of the "equal time" requirement, a broadcast station that makes time available to the Republican and Democratic candidates for a particular elective office, for debate or for almost any other purpose, must make the same amount of time available to all other legally qualified candidates for that office, regardless of whether or not they are known or the size of the party (if any) they represent. In a presidential election, there frequently are ten or more minor party or independent candidates, all of whom would be legally entitled to the same amount of broadcast time provided to the Republican or Democratic candidate. While "equal time" does protect candidates against broadcaster favoritism, it also has the effect of reducing the likelihood that broadcasters will make substantial time available to major party candidates in the first place.

There were no exceptions to the original "equal time" requirements, a fact that threatened to interfere with the ability of broadcast stations even to report on the activities of candidates in newscasts. The problem became evident in 1959, when Lar "America First" Daly, a perennial candidate for office in Illinois who had taken to wearing a red, white, and blue "Uncle Sam" suit in all his public appearances, entered himself in both the Republican and Democratic primaries for mayor of Chicago. Daly soon noticed at least five newscasts in which the leading Republican and Democratic candidates (including the incumbent mayor) were seen welcoming foreign dignitaries, inaugurating a March of Dimes drive, or campaigning. Daly argued to the Federal Communications Commission (FCC) that these appearances of his opponents entitled him to "equal time"—and the FCC agreed.[11]

The Lar Daly case convinced Congress that Section 315 should be modified to exempt from the "equal time" requirement appearances by candidates in certain types of broadcast coverage. Thus, the appearance of a candidate in a "bona fide newscast," "bona fide news interview," "bona fide news documentary," or "on the spot coverage of bona fide news events" would no longer fall under the "equal time" requirement.[12] By this modification, Congress hoped to avoid inhibiting the broadcast news coverage of political campaigns, while retaining the principle of "equal time" for those broadcast exposures of a candidate subject largely to the candidate's own control.[13] This distinction was to provide the basis for the 1976 presidential debates, when the FCC ruled that debates organized by a nonpartisan entity independent of the broadcasters would be "bona fide news events" exempt from "equal time."

In the 1920s and 1930s, however, little of this could be foreseen, and political debates and potential "equal time" problems were on few, if any, minds. Radio continued to saturate the country, and the development of television was begun without broadcast debates between political candidates. The debate format was popular in radio programming, however. Programs such as "American Forum of the Air," which featured moderator Theodore Granik and two speakers, often members of Congress who confronted each other on public questions, and "America's Town Meeting of the Air," which featured two or more speakers who responded to questions from the studio audience, reached millions of listeners weekly. There also were signs of political awareness of the possibilities of a broadcast debate. During the 1936 Landon-Roosevelt election contest, Arthur Vandenberg produced a fake debate with Roosevelt by editing together excerpts from Roosevelt's speeches followed by responses prepared by Vandenberg; the "debate" was broadcast by a number of radio stations.[14] Four years later, in a speech accepting the Republican presidential nomination, Wendell Willkie issued the first debate challenge to an incumbent president; Roosevelt declined, however, claiming that he was too busy running the country to participate in campaign events, including debates.[15]

The first notable broadcast political debate—between Thomas E. Dewey and Harold Stassen—was during the 1948 Republican presidential primary campaign in Oregon. Dewey, who at that point was trailing in the primary, at first had resisted Stassen's debate challenge. When he finally accepted, Dewey dictated the terms of the confrontation. While Stassen wanted a live audience, Dewey insisted that the debate be held in a Portland, Oregon, radio studio without an audience; while Stassen had wanted to discuss a number of issues, Dewey insisted that the debate cover only the issue of outlawing communism. The debate was broadcast to a national audience by the ABC, CBS, NBC, and Mutual radio networks. Dewey won the primary by a narrow margin, and his victory generally was believed to have eliminated Stassen from the presidential race.

According to contemporary press accounts, the Dewey-Stassen debate received low marks on both oratorical style and substance. One newspaper, for example, called the proceedings a "Debate of Tweedledum and Tweedledee."[16] At the same time, however, the debate provided a glimpse of the potential of this type of encounter between candidates for a major office. As the *Washington Star* commented:

> If judgment as to the winner of last night's debate remains a matter of personal and divided opinion, there should be no disagreement on the value of such debates. They are educational in character, they put the speakers on their mettle, they reveal weaknesses which are obscured in ordinary campaign speech-making. If there were more of them, we would have better campaigns, candidates better prepared to discuss the real issues of the day and an electorate composed of the American radio public, better able to judge both issues and candidates.[17]

As television began to replace radio as the medium of choice of candidates wishing to take their case to the public through broadcasting, the potential of radio political debates was soon forgotten. Television receivers were becoming common fixtures in American homes, and television had made its political presence known in gavel-to-gavel coverage of the 1952 nominating conventions. In 1950, about 4.5 million American families, or about 11 percent of the nation's households, owned television sets; by 1960, this number had swollen to 44 million families, or about 88 percent of the nation's households.[18]

The first specific suggestion for televised debates between presidential candidates generally is attributed to Senator Blair Moody of Michigan. Senator Moody had been the Washington correspondent for *The Detroit News* before his election to the Senate, and retained his interest in the news media. In an appearance on the CBS radio program, "The People's Platform," in July 1952, Senator Moody proposed a televised debate in the coming campaign between Governor Adlai Stevenson and General Dwight Eisenhower:

> I think I should like to make a suggestion that you might . . . be interested in. You know television and radio have remade the American political

scene. People now are sitting in on conventions where the candidates can talk to the people even though they can't get around on different stops to see them all. I think it might be very good for CBS or NBC or someone to put on a series of debates between General Eisenhower and Governor Stevenson. I think that it would be a very good idea . . . because I would like to hear the relative views of these two men contrasted with each other.[19]

The networks quickly responded. NBC wired the candidates offering to provide time for debate if they would agree to participate; CBS extended a similar invitation shortly thereafter, although it expressed its opinion that for the debate to be feasible Congress would have to suspend or revoke the "equal time" provision. Both candidates declined the networks' offers. Eisenhower's media advisor counseled that "a flat and abrupt turn down" would be in the general's best interests, while Stevenson appeared unsure and perhaps disdainful of this possible use of television.

Despite the candidates' reluctance, the networks continued to be intrigued by the idea of televised presidential debates for at least two reasons. First, because the debates would be an important national event, they would be likely to attract large audiences; this could both enhance the medium's image as a news source and generate public interest in other television programming. Second, the idea of a debate between the candidates of the major political parties might be used as a wedge to convince Congress to eliminate or substantially alter the "equal time" provision that had been a continual annoyance to the broadcast industry. The networks, lead by Frank Stanton of CBS and Robert Sarnoff of NBC, saw the proposed televised presidential debates as a means of convincing Congress that as a practical matter these programs would be possible only if equal time did not have to be given to the many minor party candidates. The networks hoped that the programs would be sufficiently important to warrant repeal of Section 315.

In the following years, the networks seized every opportunity to remind Congress that televised presidential debates were possible only if Section 315 did not stand in the way. In 1955, Stanton offered to provide free time on CBS radio and television networks for the broadcast of a debate-type program featuring the two major party presidential candidates if Congress would amend the law so that free time would not have to be given to minor party candidates. The program Stanton proposed was to have featured the candidates speaking one after the other on issues designated by six leading news reporters; the program was to be broadcast "live," but the candidates were to speak from separate locations.[20] Congress did not act on the Stanton proposal.

In the 1956 campaign, Eisenhower and Stevenson did not agree to appear jointly on radio and television. Stevenson had engaged in a nationally televised debate with Estes Kefauver in the Florida presidential primary, an appearance Stevenson had felt compelled to make because Kefauver had won the Minnesota primary, and it was believed that all of the spring primaries would depend on the Florida results. The debate was widely received as extremely dull and probably indecisive. Although he won the primary, Stevenson seemed to come away from the Florida experience with little enthusiasm for another debate. Eisenhower, who still enjoyed immense personal popularity, was disinclined to share it with Stevenson in a televised joint appearance.

The First Televised Presidential Debate: Kennedy-Nixon

As the 1960 presidential election approached, NBC proposed a plan for a series of eight programs about the election. Six of the programs would feature a joint appearance by the Democratic and Republican presidential candidates; one program would be a joint appearance of the Democratic and Republican vice-presidential candidates; and the eighth program would feature the minor party candidates. The network proposed to accomplish this by expanding its highly regarded "Meet the Press" program from one-half hour to one hour and by rescheduling it on Saturday evening during prime television viewing hours. Since "Meet the Press" was a "bona fide news interview," the network believed it had found a way around the "equal time" law.

At about the same time, further impetus for televised presidential debates came from Adlai Stevenson. Although he had not been eager to debate Eisenhower in the preceding elections, Stevenson apparently had concluded that televised debates would improve future campaigns. In an article in *This Week* magazine entitled "Plan for a Great Debate," Stevenson suggested that each week from Labor Day to election eve all of the networks should broadcast ninety-minute programs featuring the presidential candidates of the two major parties. Under his proposal, each program would deal with a separate broad issue, and each would provide for the statement of a position by one candidate and a response by the other candidate. Stevenson believed his plan would offer the following benefits:

> Sustained, serious discussion on all networks would reach all the people directly. It would require effort on their part, mental effort, and I know of no better cure for apathy. It would end the financial problem that TV now presents to the parties. It would end the tendency to reduce everything to assertions and slogans. It would diminish the temptation of politicians to entertain, to please and evade the unpleasant realities.[21]

The growing interest in televised encounters between presidential candidates led to renewed discussion in Congress of the possibility of suspending, altering, or revoking the "equal time" provision. CBS proposed that Congress suspend Section 315 for presidential and vice-presidential candidates to allow the networks to offer free time to the Democratic and Republican presidential candidates in the coming election.

While the issue of televised presidential debates was being argued, John F. Kennedy and Hubert H. Humphrey, candidates for the Democratic presidential nomination, had appeared in a televised debate during the West Virginia primary. The debate originated from a television station in Charleston, West Virginia, and was carried throughout the East Coast by an informal "network" of television stations. Taped portions of the debate later appeared on some network news programs.

In the summer of 1960, at the urging of the broadcast industry, Congress finally passed a joint resolution suspending the applicability of the "equal time" law to presidential and vice-presidential candidates until November 3, 1960.[22] On the eve of the Republican convention's nomination of Richard Nixon to face John Kennedy, who had already been nominated by the Democrats, NBC's Sarnoff wired Kennedy and Nixon an invitation to appear together on programs to be called "The Great Debates." The programs were to be part of a total of eight hours of prime evening television time to be "dedicated to a dignified, genuinely informative airing of the candidates' positions on the issues confronting our country."[23]

Kennedy was the first to accept the NBC invitation to debate, responding that the proposed programs would constitute a "notable public service in giving the American people a chance to see the candidates of the two major parties discuss the issues face-to-face."[24] Nixon responded affirmatively shortly thereafter, stating that "joint television appearances of the presidential candidates should be conducted as full and free exchanges of views without prepared texts or notes and without interruption."[25] Since ABC and CBS had made similar offers, Nixon suggested that the three networks coordinate their proposals.

The networks and the candidates met to make the arrangements for the 1960 debates. All concerned agreed that four one-hour debates would be held from September 26 to October 21 and that they would be broadcast simultaneously on all three television networks and on the four major radio networks. The programs were not to be "debates" in the traditional sense of one candidate stating a position and the other candidate countering, but rather would feature questions put to the candidates by a panel of newscasters, with the proceedings watched over by a moderator; in the first and last debate, each candidate also would make an opening and closing statement. The first debate was to be devoted to domestic issues and the last debate to foreign policy issues; the two intervening debates could address any subject the panelists chose. In three of the four debates, the candidates were to be side by side, at varying distances, in the same studios; in the third debate, however, campaign scheduling placed Kennedy in New York and Nixon in Los Angeles, and their images were joined on the television screen.

The debates clearly were a landmark in the history of political campaigning—and in radio and television broadcasting. Surveys found that 90 percent of the adult population knew about the debates well in advance of their broadcast, and most people looked forward to them with great interest.[26] The debates were viewed by approximately 100 million persons and listened to by an additional 10 million.[27] Never before had the electorate had an opportunity to see the two major party candidates for the presidency discussing their views on election issues in the same forum at the same time. The programs led to an enormous outpouring of comment, not only on the candidates, but also on this unprecedented use of television, and marked television's true coming of age as a political instrument.

The 1960 debates probably will be remembered most for the television "image" of the candidates in the first debate. Vice-President Nixon, who had been ill and was in pain from a knee injury, looked tired and pale on the television screen, with deep shadows under his eyes. Because he had declined to use professional television makeup, he also looked unshaven, and the gray suit he wore provided little contrast with the gray background of the television set. To millions of television viewers, Nixon looked "half slouched, his 'Lazy Shave' powder faintly streaked with sweat, his eyes exaggerated hollows of blackness, his jaw, jowls, and face drooping with strain."[28] In contrast, Kennedy appeared with a natural sun tan, well rested, and vigorous. To the surprise of many who had doubted his maturity or his ability to hold his own with Nixon, long regarded as a champion debater, Kennedy took the debate to Nixon and put him on the defensive. As summarized by Theodore White, "there was first and above all, the crude, overwhelming impression that side by side the two seemed evenly matched—and this even matching in the popular imagination was for Kennedy a major victory."[29]

Kennedy achieved a certain "star" status from the first debate, and his campaign crowds grew larger and more enthusiastic. Although many observers believed that Nixon "won" the second and third debates and that the final debate probably was a draw, the 1960 debates were popularly perceived as an important and perhaps decisive Kennedy "image" victory. After Kennedy was elected by an extremely small margin, he declared, "[I]t was TV more than anything else that turned the tide."[30]

After Kennedy-Nixon: Fading Hopes

The Kennedy-Nixon debates made televised encounters between candidates the hottest thing in electioneering since the campaign button. Federal, state, and local candidates everywhere pursued debates with their opponents in the next few years, while local broadcasters, eager for the prestige and large audiences that might result from debates, pursued the candidates. The debates also were copied in the next elections in a number of foreign countries, including Germany, Sweden, Finland, Italy, and Japan.[31]

President Kennedy, meanwhile, had indicated that he would appear on television with his Republican opponent in 1964. A Presidential Commission on Campaign Costs, formed to suggest ways of stemming the increasing costs of campaigning, had recommended, among other measures, "that Section 315 . . . be suspended in the same form as in 1960 for the 1964 general election," which would make debates possible again without "equal time" problems. With Kennedy's support, a bill to do just that had passed both houses of Congress and had been referred to a conference committee to work out the few differences in the versions passed by each body. Before the committee completed its work, however, Kennedy was assassinated.[32]

With Kennedy's death, the possibility of recurring televised presidential debates faded. Lyndon B. Johnson had no interest in debating Barry Goldwater in 1964 and, therefore, made sure that the Democratic-controlled Congress did not complete the proposed suspension of Section 315. The Republicans pursued the possibility of a debate nonetheless and offered to pay half the cost of purchasing television time for the event. (Had the major parties paid for their TV exposure, any minor party seeking "equal time" would have had to pay also, which minor parties generally are unable to do.) This offer was refused by President Johnson, who knew he was far ahead of Goldwater in the polls and saw no reason to risk a debate. NBC offered the candidates and their vice-presidential running mates an opportunity to appear together on a number of its "Meet the Press" programs, but this offer also was rejected by Johnson.

In 1968, televised debates returned to the primaries. While conducting a whirlwind campaign for the Democratic nomination, Robert Kennedy had hoped to avoid debating either Eugene McCarthy or Hubert Humphrey, the two other leading contenders for the nomination. But when McCarthy won the Oregon primary in the week before the crucial California primary, Kennedy saw no way to avoid McCarthy's challenge to a televised debate. The two candidates accepted ABC's invitation to appear together on a special presentation of "Issues and Answers," a program that originated from ABC's studio in San Francisco. In keeping with the program's regular format, the candidates were questioned by a panel of news reporters. The "debate" attracted 32 million viewers nationally and outdrew the entertainment programming of the other two networks, but was labeled "tepid" by the press. Kennedy won the California primary the next day by a narrow margin.

The assassination of Robert Kennedy left the California delegation to the Democratic convention uncommitted. The delegation invited McCarthy, Humphrey, and George McGovern to appear together before it and to debate their campaign positions; the delegation also invited the television cameras. Although the event had little political impact because it came on the eve of the nomination—and the California delegation's vote already was virtually committed to Humphrey—the way the debate was set up was similar to that used in the 1976 presidential debates. By its decision to hold a debate, to invite the candidates to participate, and to offer broadcasters an opportunity to cover it as a "news event," the California delegation took on a role similar to the role taken by the League of Women Voters eight years later.

Shortly after the Democratic convention, the director of the Eagleton Institute of Politics at Rutgers University suggested in a letter to *The New York Times* that

> a civic group or some national organization could invite Humphrey and Nixon under mutually agreed ground rules to engage in one or more debates. The networks would then be free to make a determination of the news value of such confrontations and cover or not cover them as they might wish.[33]

As it turned out, the suggestion was before its time.

Richard Nixon had not forgotten the narrow margin by which he had lost the 1960 election, nor the fact that many observers had attributed the loss to the first of the televised debates with John Kennedy. In 1968, with a lead in the polls, Nixon had no intention of debating Hubert Humphrey, and he was particularly anxious to avoid giving added exposure to third-party candidate George Wallace, whom Humphrey was urging be included in any debate. Senate Republicans first delayed and then blocked the proposed legislation that again would have suspended Section 315—and made debates difficult to avoid. Although Humphrey may not have been particularly anxious to debate either, for he lacked the unique Kennedy skill with television and must have been concerned at the prospect of defending the incumbent administration's Vietnam policies in debate, he did challenge Nixon to debate and even offered to pay for the television time. But Nixon successfully dodged this proposal and many others from a variety of would-be debate promoters, ranging from the National Press Club in Washington, D.C., to the owner of the Astrodome in Houston, Texas.

The election of 1972 would not feature televised presidential debates either. In this election, President Nixon was so far ahead in the polls that political experts believed George McGovern could win only if a miracle occurred, and the incumbent president showed no inclination to risk a televised debate that might provide McGovern with that miracle. Congress had passed campaign reform legislation that, among other things, repealed the "equal time" law for presidential and vice-presidential candidates, but President Nixon had vetoed that measure, and the campaign reform legislation later enacted did not include a repeal of "equal time."

The networks had sought to find a way around "equal time" during the 1972 primary campaign by using their "bona fide news interview programs"—"Face the Nation," "Issues and Answers," and "Meet the Press"—for joint "debate" appearances by Democratic primary candidates Humphrey and McGovern. The length of the programs was expanded to one hour and their normal broadcast times were changed from mid-afternoon to early evening. After the broadcast of the first program, however, Congresswoman Shirley Chisholm of New York and Mayor Sam Yorty of Los Angeles, both of whom also were candidates for the Democratic nomination, filed complaints with the FCC charging that the "debate" format and the length and time changes had made the programs no longer exempt from "equal time" and, therefore, that the networks were required to provide "equal opportunities." Although the FCC ruled that the programs had remained exempt and that other candidates were not entitled to "equal time," a reviewing federal court issued a preliminary order directing CBS to give Congresswoman Chisholm one half-hour of broadcast time and instructing ABC to include her in a scheduled "Issues and Answers" program with candidates Humphrey and McGovern or to give her equivalent time. The preliminary order did not constitute a final ruling on the issue of whether the network interview programs could be rescheduled and used for joint appearances without loss of their "equal time" exemption, but the litigation never went further, and the preliminary order discouraged other efforts of this kind.[34]

As Richard Nixon savored a landslide victory in 1972, the next election seemed particularly distant. Given the problems of "equal time" and the length of time that had elapsed since the last televised presidential debates, the reemergence of such debates in 1976 appeared almost as unlikely as the possibility that a scandal would drive the newly reelected president from office.

Carter-Ford: Making History Again

The 1976 televised presidential debates took place because of a unique combination of factors. First, as a result of the Watergate scandal during the Nixon administration, the public seemed to wish to scrutinize the candidates more closely than they had in the past, and the candidates felt greater pressure to engage in "open" campaigning. Second, although Gerald Ford was the incumbent presidential candidate, he had not been elected to the presidency or even to the vice-presidency and so was not regarded as a true incumbent, a man who could claim an existing public mandate. Third, neither Ford nor Jimmy Carter could be confident of victory; although the campaign began with Carter far ahead in the polls, he had not been a national figure, and was viewed as an "unknown," and his support, therefore, was perceived as "soft." Finally, in a controversial ruling in 1975, the FCC had held that radio and television stations could broadcast debates between the Democratic and Republican contenders without incurring "equal time" obligations to minor party candidates as long as the broadcasters had not arranged the events.

The history of the 1975 FCC ruling begins in 1962, when a radio station in Detroit broadcast a debate between the Republican and Democratic candidates for the office of governor of Michigan. The debate had been arranged by the Detroit Economic Club, a nonpartisan association of business, civic, and governmental leaders that had sponsored similar debates in past elections. After the broadcast, the candidate of the Socialist Labor party requested equal time from the station, which refused the request on the grounds that the broadcast had been "on-the-spot coverage of a bona fide news event" exempt from Section 315 under the 1959 "Lar Daly amendments." In response to a complaint filed by the party, the FCC held that the debate was not a "bona fide news event." Where the appearance of a candidate was not simply incidental to an otherwise newsworthy event, said the commission, and where the event itself was planned and staged, Congress had not intended the "bona fide news event" exemption to apply.[35]

The FCC reached the same conclusion in another decision that same year. The Prohibition party had sought "equal time" from NBC and CBS following the networks' broadcast of a debate between the candidates for governor of California. The debate had been arranged by United Press International (UPI) as part of the program for a UPI convention. "Where the appearance of a candidate is designed by him to serve his own political advantage . . ." the commission ruled, "such program cannot be considered to be on-the-spot coverage of a bona fide news event simply because the broadcaster deems that the candi-

date's appearance . . . will be . . . newsworthy." It made no difference, the commission noted, whether the debate was arranged by
the broadcaster or by a third party.[36] As the FCC later acknowledged,
these two rulings had the effect of "virtually eliminating the possibility
that such debates would receive further broadcast coverage."[37]

In 1975, however, responding to a petition submitted by the Aspen
Institute Program on Communications and Society, the FCC reversed
its two earlier decisions; it now exempted from the "equal time" requirement debates between candidates in situations "presenting the
same factual contexts" as had the earlier cases. The commission concluded that its position that an event could not be a "bona fide news
event" if a candidate's appearance was a central aspect of the event
had been inconsistent with Congress's intent in adopting the "bona fide
news event" exemption in 1959.[38] The effect of the FCC's reversal was
to allow broadcasters to carry debates between some candidates without having to provide "equal time" to all other candidates for the same
office, but only if the debates were: (1) arranged by a party not associated with the broadcaster; (2) carried live and in their entirety;
and (3) reasonably could be considered newsworthy in all other re-
spects and not for the purpose of giving political advantage to any
candidate.[39]

The *Aspen* decision was seen by some critics as improperly usurping
Congress's role in legislating the limits of "equal time," while other
critics charged that it would unfairly disadvantage minor party candidates. "The Bicentennial political broadcast model which the Aspen
Institute gave us," one critic wrote, "is a grand step toward establishment of the Democratic and Republican parties in a two party political
system. Our founding fathers would not have approved the model."[40]
Still others saw the decision as a partisan ploy by the Republican-con-
trolled agency to favor the incumbent Republican president.[41] A federal court upheld the FCC's decision, however, and the Supreme Court
let that decision stand.[42]

It remained only for some organization to arrange a debate between
presidential candidates and to invite broadcast coverage. The League
of Women Voters, a nonprofit, nonpartisan organization with a long
history of voter education activities, quickly got a headstart on possible competitors for this role by taking over, through its Education
Fund, a newly organized effort of the Public Broadcasting System
(PBS) and citizen organizers (particularly Charles Benton of the Benton Foundation) to hold a series of televised "Presidential Forums"
during the 1976 preliminaries.[43] Seven of the contenders for the Democratic presidential nomination, including Jimmy Carter, had participated in the first forum in Boston in February 1976. The event featured a
statement on a designated campaign issue by each of the candidates

and comments on the statement by the other candidates. It was broadcast nationally by the PBS television network and by radio stations affiliated with the National Public Radio network. Three other televised forums were held at other locations during the primaries.

While the forums were still under way, the League began planning for a series of debates between the Republican and Democratic candidates for president. League chapters throughout the country circulated petitions among the public calling on the candidates to debate and encouraged editorial support in the press. Immediately after Gerald Ford's nomination, the League wired Ford and Jimmy Carter a formal proposal for a series of debates under the League's sponsorship.

Both candidates already had decided to debate. In his nomination acceptance speech, Ford inserted what was intended as a surprise challenge: "I am ready, I am eager to go before the American people and debate the real issues, face to face, with Jimmy Carter." At almost the same moment, mimeograph machines at Carter's headquarters in Atlanta were duplicating a Carter challenge to Ford. Shortly after the Ford speech, Robert Dole, the Republican vice-presidential candidate, issued a debate challenge to Walter Mondale, his Democratic counterpart.

Although patterned closely on the 1960 debates, the 1976 encounters made history in their own right. They marked the first time an incumbent president met face to face with a challenger to debate campaign issues, and they included the first debate between vice-presidential candidates. Once again, the televised events became the focal point of the campaign, attracting enormous audiences, considerable press commentary, and virtually endless assessments of which candidate had "won" the debates and the impact of the debates on the outcome of the election.

While the 1960 debates were widely remembered for the "images" they delivered, particularly Richard Nixon's poor television appearance in the first debate, "image" played a lesser role in 1976. Although Carter appeared nervous and deferential in the first debate, the image of neither candidate disturbed viewers' expectations. Instead, the 1976 debates probably will be remembered most for the first major substantive "slip" in televised presidential debates.

In the middle of the second debate, President Ford was asked about his support for the Helsinki Agreement, a treaty criticized by some as guaranteeing the absence of any challenge to Soviet control of Eastern European nations such as Rumania, Poland, and Czechoslovakia. Ford defended the agreement as a means of peacekeeping and then stated: "There is no Soviet domination of Eastern Europe, and there never will be under a Ford administration." In a follow-up question, he was asked: "Did I understand you to say, sir, that the Russians are not using Eastern Europe as their own sphere of influence in occupying most of the countries there, and making sure with their troops that it's a

Communist zone . . . ?'' At this point, the president interrupted to reaffirm his view that the Eastern European countries "do not consider themselves dominated by the Soviet Union."

What the president later indicated he had meant to say was that the Helsinki Agreement simply reflected a Soviet domination that was a practical fact of life but that the United States supported the desire of the citizens of the Eastern European countries to be independent. His comments, however, were not so interpreted. Taking advantage of the opening, Carter responded: "I would like to see Mr. Ford convince the Polish-Americans and the Czech-Americans and the Hungarian-Americans . . . that those countries don't live under the domination and the supervision of the Soviet Union. . . ." The press also jumped on the president's comments; the president's position on Eastern Europe, or more precisely the question of whether the president knew what he was talking about, suddenly became a major campaign issue, one that was resolved only after Ford finally admitted he had misspoken.[44]

Despite Carter's nervousness in the first debate and Ford's difficulty with the Eastern Europe matter in the second, both candidates believed their causes had benefited. The Ford staff believed that the debates prevented the voters from committing themselves to Carter, who had achieved an early lead, and had demonstrated overall that Ford was competent. Indeed, Ford stated: "I believe that they [the debates] ought to be an institution in future Presidential campaigns. I really believe that."[45] The Carter staff believed that the debates had helped to detract attention from their candidate's campaign difficulties, including an ill-advised interview in *Playboy* magazine, and had given him credibility as a potential president.[46] Carter himself said on the day after his narrow victory:

> If it hadn't been for the debates, I would have lost. They established me as competent on foreign and domestic affairs and gave the viewers reason to think Jimmy Carter has something to offer.[47]

But as of this writing, President Carter has not said whether he intends to be the first elected incumbent president to debate an opponent on radio and television.

III/The Impact of Televised Debates

Candidates, especially presidential candidates, spend millions of dollars buying television time, generally without knowing what—except, perhaps, a large audience—they are getting for their money. Indeed, candidates are notorious for trying any and every available election technique in the hope that it might work, even if there is no evidence that it does. As with other forms of television exposure of candidates, the actual impact of televised debates is not fully known. For example, were John Kennedy and Jimmy Carter correct when they ascribed their election victories to televised debates? Have debates informed voters about important campaign issues? about the candidates' personalities? Do debates affect the way the public votes?

Social scientists have not reached firm conclusions about the effects of televised presidential debates. There have only been two series of these debates, and they have come about with too little advance notice in both cases to have been studied as carefully as the experts would prefer. Moreover, it probably is impossible in any case to isolate the impact of televised debates from the impact of other forms of television exposure. In 1960, for example, John Kennedy delivered a speech to a meeting of Protestant ministers in Houston in an effort to meet the issue of his Catholicism head-on. The reaction to the local telecast of the speech was so favorable that it was edited into a one-half hour film and broadcast in ten key, undecided states; in each state, Kennedy outpolled Nixon in the election.[1]

Furthermore, the effect of television exposure cannot be separated with any assurance from the effect of other communications sources, including the voter's family and friends and the newspapers and magazines the voter reads. A voter receives information and images from all of these sources, and television clearly does not act "like a hypodermic stimulus on an inert subject."[2]

41

Newspaper accounts of the televised debates, for example, may have as much impact on voters as the debates themselves.[3] One study of the first debate in 1976 concluded that, although the reaction of viewers to both candidates generally was favorable, the public tended to perceive the candidates less favorably after reading critiques of the debates by reporters.[4]

While it may not be possible to determine the effects of televised presidential debates with precision, some general conclusions are possible.

Audience Attraction

The debates have placed the candidates before the largest audience in history, audiences that could be reached in no other way. Although imprecise and perhaps somewhat contradictory, the many estimates of the audience reached by the 1960 and 1976 debates paint a remarkable picture. In 1960:

- between 85 million and 120 million people saw or heard at least one of the debates;[5]

- 70 million adults saw or heard the first debate;[6]

- 55 percent of the adults in the country saw or heard *each* debate;[7]

- 90 percent of all families owning television sets watched at least a portion of one debate, and more than 25 percent watched at least a portion of *all four* debates.[8]

Although paid political programs generally *lose* 30 percent of the audience of the programs they replace, the debates drew audiences that were 20 percent higher than those for the popular, prime-time entertainment programs the debates replaced.[9] As Theodore White observed, "no larger assembly of human beings, their minds focused on one problem, has ever happened in history."[10]

The 1976 figures are no less impressive:

- an average of 87 million persons saw at least part of the debates;[11]

- 64 million *households* saw one or more of the debates, and the average household watched 2.8 of the debates;[12]

- 100 million to 120 million persons saw at least part of the first debate;[13]

- 89 percent of all registered voters saw or heard the first debate;[14]

- 83 percent of the adult population saw or heard at least one debate.[15]

These extremely high audience figures remained fairly constant throughout the debates, suggesting that the debates have a unique ability not only to attract but also to hold an audience. A. C. Nielsen surveys, for example, indicated a total audience, for each average minute of each of the three presidential debates, of 70 million, 64 million, and 63 million viewers, respectively, a drop of only 10 percent during the series.[16] Nielsen figures also indicated that each debate program lost only about 10 percent of its viewers during its course. This appears consistent with a 1960 study that found that the average family watching a debate viewed 54 minutes of the 60-minute program.[17]

Voter Interest and Turnout

The large audiences that view televised debates appear to become more interested in the election campaign and the candidates. In 1960, for example:

> The drama of the event [the first debate] caused repercussions everywhere. Money began to pour into both campaign headquarters. Crowds grew larger and more emotional, almost hysterical in some cases. Serious discussion of the issues increased. Campaign workers hustled voters with renewed vigor. . . .[18]

Studies of the 1976 debates confirm that they, too, increased voter interest and caused voters to pay more attention to the election campaign.[19] It is unclear, however, whether this interest leads to a higher voter turnout at the polls. The fact that more than 63 percent of eligible voters went to the polls in 1960 following the debates, and that this represented one of the heaviest votes ever, may indicate a correlation between televised debate and voter turnout. But the 1960 turnout was only about 1 percent higher than the turnout of eligible voters in 1952 and 2 percent higher than the turnout in 1964.[20] The 1976 debates, while sometimes credited with contributing to a higher than expected vote, did not stop the downward trend in voting; only 54 percent of eligible voters went to the polls that year compared to the 55 percent voting in the Nixon landslide of 1972.[21]

Candidate Images

Televised debates have demonstrated their ability to convey the "image" or personality of the presidential candidates. Surveys of the 1960 debates disclosed that it was the "image" of the candidates that most interested or impressed viewers.[22] When the debate seemed to lead to a clash of personalities, the public apparently was particularly interested.[23] In determining who had "won" the debates, the most important determinant seemed to be the "style" of a candidate (whether he appeared knowledgeable and responded to questions without seeming evasive) and his personality (whether he appeared sincere, honest, and energetic).[24]

The 1960 debates are reported to have caused an actual change in the public perception of the two candidates. The image of John Kennedy is said to have changed from "an eager, affable, young and ambitious political aspirant into one that epitomized the competent, dynamic and quick-thinking candidate." On the other hand, Richard Nixon was perceived before the debates as an experienced, "tough" politician and a master debater (a veteran of the "Kitchen Debate" with Soviet Premier Khrushchev), but the debates changed his image among some viewers to that of a nervous, complex, and somewhat disappointing person.[25]

The impact of the televised debates on the perception of "image" is suggested by a comparison of the reactions of persons who watched the 1960 debates on television and those who listened on radio. The latter group, unable to see and compare the faces of Nixon and Kennedy, judged Nixon to have "won" the encounters, while television viewers overwhelmingly awarded a "victory" to Kennedy.[26]

As indicated earlier, the effects of television viewing are not always the sole product of television itself, and sometimes may be more the product of what other media say *about* what is seen on the television. Newspaper accounts of the first Kennedy-Nixon debates generally identified Kennedy as having "won" the encounter, which appears to have had an impact on the opinion of the public concerning the relative performance of the candidates.[27] An even clearer example of this relationship between the media, however, was the Ford "slip" on Eastern Europe in the second of the 1976 debates. In a poll taken for the Ford campaign immediately after that debate, 44 percent of those polled reported that Ford had "won" the debate, while 43 percent favored Carter. But by midnight the next day, after newspapers had reported that Ford had committed a blunder, only 17 percent of the same sample believed Ford had performed better in the debate and 62 percent then favored Carter.[28] In the face of contrary press reports, many viewers did not trust their own perceptions of the candidates.

Nonetheless, the apparent ability of televised debates to convey candidate images has resulted in concern in some quarters that the debates overemphasize image at the expense of issues. "Debates," it has been said, "reinforce the power of entertainment values in politics [and] accelerate the trend to personalism."[29] In a 1964 report, a Commission on Presidential Campaign Debates established by the American Political Science Association warned that "the choice of Presidential candidates must not be limited to those who are masters of appearance on television.''[30] And even before the 1976 debates began, a panel of four experienced politicians told *Newsweek* readers to expect encounters that would expose the candidates' images, personalities, and styles, but little in the way of their ideas or the campaign issues.[31]

While the fear that presidential debates might become simply a contest of slickly packaged images is a valid one, presidential elections have emphasized images for years, and the promotion of image is not unique to this type of television presentation or to television itself. Candidates are seeking to convey the image they want when they organize political rallies, wave from the back of a railroad car, or hold a press conference for the purported purpose of announcing a position on an "issue." Contemporary accounts suggest that even in the Lincoln-Douglas debates the images of the candidates may have made a greater impression than their arguments. Douglas' fierce demeanor and powerful voice and Lincoln's awkward but magnetic appearance were of great interest to those attending or reading about the debates, just as television viewers in 1960 were fascinated with Richard Nixon's poor television image during his first debate.[32]

It would be a mistake to conclude that conveying an image has no legitimate role in a presidential election, especially where the image conveyed is a reasonably accurate reflection of the candidate. The ability to project a television image allows a candidate to overcome inaccurate public perceptions of the candidate or even deep-seated biases. In 1960, for example, John Kennedy used the debates effectively to correct public perception of him as too young and inexperienced to be a national leader, as well as to overcome an anti-Catholic bias. In 1976, Jimmy Carter used the debates to counter what his aides called the "weirdo" image and to overcome an anti-South bias.[33] Similarly, Gerald Ford used the debates to help refute a public image that tagged him as "dumb" despite his excellent educational background.

If the public ever had a tendency to believe everything it saw on television, it has long since learned not to. The collective wisdom gained from years of exposure to expensive "spot" advertising for products and candidates, both of which sometimes fail to perform as advertised, has developed a public resistance to the packaged "media candidate," a resistance that should not be underestimated. While candidates have controlled the debates to some extent (by choosing the formats and by simply ignoring questions they do not want to answer), they do not control them in the same way they control paid political advertising. Thus, the image of a candidate conveyed by a television debate is likely to be a reasonably accurate reflection of the candidate. Walter Cronkite once remarked that "television . . . can detect insincerity as quickly as a more orthodox X-ray can detect a broken bone."[34] In a similar vein, commenting specifically on televised debates, Norman Cousins has observed:

No amount of TV makeup can change the way a man's eyes move, or the way his lips are drawn under surges of animus or temper. When the camera burrows into a man's face, the fact that some wrinkles may be covered up by pancake makeup is not as important as the visibility of the emotions that come to the surface. The strength of the TV debates derives less from what is hidden than from what is impossible to conceal.[35]

Campaign Issues

Televised presidential debates do indeed, notwithstanding charges to the contrary, convey information about campaign issues. Voters have turned to televised debates as a source of information about campaign issues and believe they have gotten what they came for. According to a 1976 survey, the debates that year were used more than any other medium, including newspapers and magazines, as a source of information about campaign issues.[36] Another study found that between 50 and 70 percent of the voters questioned believed they had learned where the candidates stood on at least some issues by viewing the debates. Still another study found that, while debates indeed were rated by viewers as helpful in judging the personalities of the candidates, the viewers also reported learning the candidates' stands on issues and what the candidates would do if elected.[37]

Moreover, the studies confirm that voters are right to believe that they derive information from the debates. A survey conducted for Gerald Ford in 1976, for example, found that on issues discussed during the first debate (amnesty for draft resisters and use of government funds or private sector investment to stimulate the economy), "significant movement occurred from pre-debate 'don't know' and 'it depends' responses to post-debate identification of Ford and Carter as for or against each issue."[38] Similarly, another study of the 1976 debates found that viewers' knowledge about the candidates increased with each succeeding debate.[39] The 1960 debates had a similar impact, increasing public awareness of issues such as U.S. policy on Quemoy and Matsu, the country's international prestige, unemployment, and medical insurance.[40] An empirical assessment of the debates concluded that "in general . . . the debates clearly performed one of their major manifest tasks, that of providing information about the candidates and their issue positions that was new to many voters."[41]

The importance of televised debates as a source of information about issues and candidate positions becomes evident when considered in conjunction with charges that similar information is not contained in network television news coverage. A leading study of the 1972 elections concluded that the network news programs were almost devoid of discussions of candidate qualifications, but concentrated in-

stead on the "hoopla" of electioneering—motorcades, crowds, heck-
lers, and rallies. According to the study, steady viewers of television
learned almost nothing from television news about candidates' positions on issues and actually got more useful information from the often
criticized paid political spots.[42]

A *Wall Street Journal* reporter assigned to learn about the 1976 California primary by watching television news in a Los Angeles hotel
room similarly concluded that "most political coverage was superfi-
cial. A typical report would show a candidate shaking hands in crowds,
present a brief excerpt from a speech, and then show the candidate
saying he expects to do well in California. . . ."[43] If these observations are accurate, it may explain why the public has been so attracted
to televised debates not only for an image of a candidate but also for
information about campaign issues.

Voting Behavior

For a candidate, the question of whether the debates interest the
public in an election, convey images, or provide information is second-
ary to the question of whether the debates influence the way in which a
vote is cast. Social scientists long ago reached the general consensus,
however, that the mass media of communications, including television,
have very little ability to persuade people to change their votes.[44]

Research indicates that as many as 80 percent of the voters may
have chosen their candidate before an election campaign even begins
and that very few of them change their minds.[45] Those who choose
early, as well as many who do make their voting decisions during the
campaign, make their choice largely on the basis of their political party
affiliation or preference; their general liberal/conservative position, the
existing "image" of a candidate; and their personal interaction with
family, friends, and associates.[46] They tend to seek out media content
favorable to the candidate they prefer and to avoid or unconsciously
reject information favorable to the candidates they oppose.[47]

Although mass media in general rarely sway votes, they do have an
important impact on elections. There is considerable evidence that
television and other media tend to reinforce voter intentions, crystal-
lize the predisposition formed from the influences noted above, and
prevent wavering. These are the same functions generally performed
by political rallies with speeches, bands, and balloons—literally rally-
ing a candidate's supporters to stay with him and to fulfill their basic
voting intent.[48] Thus, the more often people see the candidate they
tend to prefer on television or read about the candidate in the press, the
more committed they tend to become to voting for that candidate.[49] In
sum, "the mass media's role is primarily one of reinforcing basic voter

loyalties. . . ."[50] This reinforcement can determine the outcome of an election if it convinces people to vote who might not have done so or if it prevents defections.

The impact of televised presidential debates on the electorate has followed the pattern of other forms of mass communications. Studies indicate that a viewer's reaction to the debates depended on the viewer's preexisting attitudes about his political party and the candidates; as with other media presentations, the debates generally reinforced political predispositions and did not change votes.[51]

The popular belief that the 1960 debates so swayed voters as to win the election for Kennedy has not been proven; voter preference polls that year never changed more than 1 percent in the period before, during, and after the debates, and even this small change cannot be attributed with any assurance to the debates.[52] A leading study of the impact of the 1960 debates by Samuel Lubell concluded:

> One cannot isolate with precision the influence of the TV debates from all other factors which shaped the vote. One can only advance a judgment as to their effect. My own judgment is that the debates did not bring any basic change in the voting pattern of the nation. In the end the vote pretty well matched the mood of the nation as it stood before the debates began.[53]

The debates instead "resulted primarily in a strengthening of commitment to one's own party and candidate."[54] Very few voters switched their candidate allegiance in 1960, and those who did generally were acting consistently with their past voting inclinations. John Kennedy benefited from the debates to the degree that they confirmed or crystallized the vote of Democrats who had not been firmly committed to him and who might not have voted at all without this reinforcement.[55] In practical terms, this meant that Democratic voters were convinced that they should stick with the Democratic candidate despite their original doubts about his religion and maturity. Given the closeness of the Kennedy victory, this "strengthening of commitment" could well have been decisive.

The 1976 debates followed the same pattern. Polls by CBS and NBC found that few voters reported actually changing their voting predisposition because of the debates.[56] At the same time, however, Jimmy Carter's media experts concluded from their own experience that just as the earlier Kennedy-Nixon debates had served as "a reinforcing mechanism for those inclined to vote for Kennedy but who had doubts," so too the 1976 debates provided a forum in which voters could find reinforcement for their "soft" preference for Carter.[57] David Sears concluded from his study of the 1976 debates that they seemed to be "strongly reinforcing," bringing seriously wavering voters "home" to their voting predisposition, and even influencing voters who were undecided how to vote.[58] Once again, given the closeness of the election, the "reinforcing mechanism" might well have been decisive.[59]

Televised debates probably are more effective at crystallizing or reinforcing a vote than other types of media presentations. Most forms of political mass communication rarely reach large numbers of people or generate substantial public interest, and those being communicated with may distrust the message they receive because the communication is controlled by the candidate, or they may ignore what is being said because it is inconsistent with their own predispositions.[60] The televised debates, however, produce much larger audiences; since they are broadcast by all networks simultaneously and offer the "conflict" of competition between candidates, the debates attract viewers who do not generally watch "political" or "public affairs" programs.[61] Moreover, the debates, unlike standard political fare, are not controlled by the candidates, which means they are considered more authoritative and trustworthy.[62] Finally, only the debates provide what might be called "double exposure," the presentation of contending candidates in a manner that makes it virtually impossible for a viewer to avoid messages that might be inconsistent with the viewer's predispositions.[63]

Televised presidential debates have demonstrated an ability to attract national audiences of unparalleled size and to motivate those audiences to an interest in the election campaign. The debates are able to convey both the personality of a candidate and the candidate's stated position on important national issues. Although the debates do not appear to have the ability to change many votes, they do seem particularly effective in reinforcing or crystallizing voting predispositions resulting from party loyalty, issue commitments, preexisting opinions about candidates, or the influence of family and friends, and that reinforcement can have a decisive impact on an election.

IV/Allocating Responsibility for Future Debates

If televised presidential debates are to become a regular feature of future presidential campaigns, some person or organization must clearly assume the responsibility for presenting them. Indeed, the absence of any such organization or entity is one reason for their sporadic history.

Responsibility for the debates means seeing to it that they are held in 1980 and thereafter, or at least that the question of whether there will be debates each election year is placed on the public agenda. It also means playing a major role in determining the timing, number, and format of debates and the way in which they are to be broadcast. If past experience is any guide, however, the organizers probably will not be able to dictate the details of the events. Rather, the candidates will insist upon retaining at least a veto right over most important matters. According to one of President Ford's aides during the 1976 debates:

> Although the League of Women Voters was used as a vehicle for presenting the debates . . . they never controlled any key issue affecting the debates. As long as the Ford and Carter camps agreed on a specific subject area, there was no question as to whether or not it would happen. . . . The debates were far too crucial a factor in the Presidential elections for either side to abdicate control, except through negotiation with the other side.[1]

Responsibility for future debates also may include the responsibility for paying for them and for determining whether or which minor party or independent candidates should be included (see Chapters V and VII for separate discussions of these issues).

Over the years, the three commercial broadcast networks—ABC, CBS, and NBC—have pushed for televised debates. The networks have offered the major party presidential candidates an opportunity to appear jointly in one format or another in every presidential election since 1952, and were largely responsible for the precedent-setting televised debates in 1960. The noncommercial network, PBS, has not had so long a history of involvement in debate issues, but participated in 1960 and 1976 by carrying the debates. The simultaneous broadcast of the debates on the four networks ensures them a large audience. Because of their interest in and importance to debates, the networks perhaps are the most obvious of the groups that might be given responsibility for future debates.

There are a number of reasons for the networks' enthusiasm for televising presidential debates.

The commercial networks are in the business of selling advertising time at prices based on the number of people watching television; political conflict between the candidates for the country's highest office has shown that it can attract very large audiences. While the networks have not sold advertising time during debate programs (although at least one network wanted to in 1960), programs that produce large audiences have some carryover impact on viewing during periods when advertising is being sold. Even PBS, which does not sell advertising time, finds large audiences attractive because they prove public interest in an activity supported by tax dollars.

Moreover, the networks have used debates as a lever in their attempts to pry Section 315, the "equal time" provision, off the statute books. Debates are used by the networks as an example of what broadcasting could do to contribute to an informed electorate if Section 315 were to be repealed, and each suggestion for presidential debates has been accompanied by a request for repeal of Section 315.

The networks and their affiliates also all own television stations licensed by the FCC pursuant to the Communications Act, which makes operation in the "public interest, convenience, and necessity" a condition of the renewal of their licenses. The FCC long ago concluded that one aspect of broadcast service in the public interest is coverage of political campaigns.[2] Participation in organizing and presenting events such as presidential debates provides a "showpiece" for demonstrating operation in the public interest.

Furthermore, the networks, like most broadcasters, are anxious to be considered journalists not only for legal purposes but also in the public perception. They view the debates as part of their role as television journalists and feel that involvement in them adds to their stature as members of the press.

These motivations and the networks' apparent eagerness to present debates are a basis for giving the networks responsibility for future televised debates. In 1976, in fact, the networks attempted to wrest responsibility for the debates from the League of Women Voters. As soon as it appeared that both candidates were willing to accept the League's debate proposal, the networks attempted to obtain a congressional suspension of Section 315 to enable them to conduct the debates themselves. This infuriated the League, which already had spent a great deal of its time and money on the project, and it successfully appealed to Congress to protect its newly staked-out turf by ignoring the network request.[3]

Another basis that has been suggested for allocating responsibility for debates to the networks is that conveying information about candidates involves journalistic judgments that should be left to journalists—in this case, the network news departments. During the 1976 debates, considerable friction arose between the League and networks because the League refused to allow the networks to "cut away" during the broadcasts to "audience reaction shots" and insisted that coverage be provided by "pool" cameras alone, which meant that each network received the same pictures. The CBS network vehemently opposed this decision on journalistic principle:

> It is a long established and important journalistic principle that those who arrange an event cannot properly tell the journalists who are covering the event where to focus their attention—what to cover and what not to cover. The managers of political conventions, the sponsors of a press interview, demonstrators—almost everybody involved as subjects when there are cameras and microphones present—are often eager to control just where the cameras and microphones are pointed and what the public will hear and see—and more important what they will not hear and see. But a reporter cannot permit such a delegation to outside parties—particularly to outside parties who are managers of, or major participants in, the event.
>
> Once the audience was there, it became part of the event and as a matter of journalistic policy, we as journalists cannot accept the direction of those who put on, or participate in, the event.[4]

NBC demanded "full journalistic rights and privileges" on the same grounds:

> News coverage . . . cannot be controlled, directly or indirectly, by the people who are being covered, or by any intermediary. If the 1976 debates are news events, they should be televised as news, by news professionals. Otherwise the whole principle of independent journalism is in jeopardy.[5]

The CBS network, charging that the League improperly had allowed the candidates to participate in the selection of the panelists for the debate programs, threatened not to cover the proceedings. The same network took the position that the subject of a news interview should have no voice in the selection of the interviewer. "We . . . will never play a game where the subjects of interviews can have any part in who's go-

:ng to interview them," observed a CBS executive, "that's pretty basic."" The League acknowledged that the candidates had been allowed to suggest panelists but denied that panelists had to appear on the candidates' lists in order to be selected. In any event, CBS did, of course, broadcast the debates—"as journalists we just couldn't ignore them."[7]

Yet another reason for giving the networks responsibility for the debates is their experience and expertise in television broadcasting. Without television, the presidential debates would lose much of their utility to the electorate. As 1976 demonstrated, the networks will broadcast the debates even if another entity has responsibility for them, but direct network responsibility may be more efficient and would ensure quality coverage.

There also are strong arguments to be made *against* allocating the responsibility for presidential debates to the television networks. First, it is important to remember that a fundamental principle of journalism is that those reporting the news should not at the same time make the news. But the organization of the joint appearance of candidates for the presidency itself makes news, just as the position taken by the candidates during the course of their appearance does. CBS anchorman and commentator Walter Cronkite made this point recently, when his televised interviews with Egyptian and Israeli leaders were said to have made news by furthering the cause of peace in the Middle East:

> It is not our job to practice diplomacy. . . . This was purely a journalistic effort. . . . We were indulging only in journalistic enterprise. And it's got to stay that way. If we became a part of the story we have lost part of our credibility.[8]

Thus, it is argued that a network that encourages candidates to debate, negotiates with the candidates the conditions of a debate, including the topics to be discussed and the panelists, if any, to appear and even the participation of third-party or independent candidates, is making the news as much as reporting it, possibly compromising the reporting of the negotiations or the event itself and threatening the network's credibility as a news organization.[9]

If responsibility for presidential debates does not rest well with a network when it is functioning as a news organization, certainly it would rest less well with the network's other major function—entertainment. Television already is frequently accused, sometimes with reason, of emphasizing entertainment values over information values when dealing with politics and government. Making presidential debates a "TV special" could trivialize the sessions and lessen their credibility.

Another argument against allocating the responsibility for continuation of presidential debates to the networks is that little public control could be exerted over their performance of this role. Although the networks have for years attempted to organize presidential debates, that does not guarantee the continuation of these efforts; indeed, circumstances may arise—lack of public interest in an election that appears one-sided, disputes among the networks over details of coverage, or fear of alienating an incumbent president or a candidate—which would lead them to abandon the project. Similarly, the networks probably are less likely than an organization such as the League of Women Voters, for example, to pursue a debate between presidential candidates other than the two major party candidates. Without both major candidates, the networks could conclude that the event was not "newsworthy" enough—and the audiences probably too small—to warrant broadcast time.

Although the networks do have an obligation under existing law and FCC policy to cover the candidates and the campaign, this obligation never has been interpreted as compelling the broadcast of particular programs, and certainly not the organization of an event for broadcast. An attempt to require the networks to sponsor presidential debates would raise difficult issues of constitutionality.

Yet another reason for avoiding network responsibility for debates is that the broadcast networks long have been charged with having too much control of mass media. Their ownership of stations and relationship with affiliates have created fears in some quarters that the nation's access to news and information is overly dependent on a few, powerful decisionmakers. Adding responsibility for presidential debates would be likely to intensify these fears because it would extend network "control" to an important part of the political and electoral process.

Any network involvement in presidential debates beyond the operation of television cameras and transmission equipment would require repeal or suspension of Section 315. As already noted, under the FCC's *Aspen* interpretation, a presidential debate is exempt from the "equal time" requirement as "on-the-spot coverage of bona fide news events" *only* if the debate is organized by an entity not associated with the broadcaster. The rationale for this limitation is that if "bona fide news events" include events staged by broadcasters, everything broadcasters choose to stage would then be "news events," allowing the networks to "stage" events when they would benefit a particular candidate, thus creating a large loophole in a law intended to prohibit use of the broadcast media to favor one candidate over another.

Section 315 was circumvented in 1976 by the role of the League of Women Voters as the nonaffiliated entity responsible for and in control of the debates. The League held the debates for the audience in attendance at the halls rented by the League, and the networks were allowed to cover the affairs as they would any other news event. While this was consistent with the FCC's *Aspen* decision, it was in many ways artificial or, as *Broadcasting* magazine labeled it, a "contrivance."[10] Although the League and everyone else knew the debates were being organized for broadcasting purposes, the League had to avoid contact with the broadcasters during the planning stages and to treat television coverage as a sidelight to the affair. This anomaly was evident in the League's instructions to debate panelists: They were to refer to the proceedings as an "event," not as "broadcasts, programs, or shows"; at the same time, the League prepared a minute-by-minute schedule for the events to ensure that their timing gave the networks the time they wanted to provide commentary before resuming regular programming.[11]

The artificiality of divorcing the broadcasters from the debates was made even more evident when the audio equipment failed during the first debate. With only a few minutes of scheduled debate remaining, the sound equipment supplied by the networks went dead, which meant that television viewers could hear nothing. The debate, supposedly held for the audience present in the hall, immediately stopped and remained stopped until the trouble could be located and repaired some 26 minutes later. The strange scene was described by Elizabeth Drew:

And then, as Carter is giving his rebuttal . . . word comes that, unbelievably, the audio has gone off, and the two candidates for the Presidency stand there silently while we wait for it to go back on. . . . The President, having been programmed to stand during the entire debate and now faced with this unforeseeable situation, remains standing. Carter, who, following the President's lead, had stood throughout the debate, at last elects to sit. . . . Assured that the cameras are not on them, the two men glance at each other and then wipe their faces. Apart from that, they do not acknowledge each other's presence; Carter, from time to time, manages a wan smile. . . . The President and the would-be President are like prisoners behind their lecterns.

Finally . . . the sound comes back on. Carter, as if he were a wound-up doll, simply resumes where he left off. . . .[12]

Marshall McLuhan remarked more colorfully that the proceedings reminded him of "two men waiting for their trousers to be pressed." The League claimed that it had tried to continue the debate in spite of the loss of television sound but that the hall's sound system had been tied in with the broadcast sound; in subsequent debates, a separate sound system was available.

The loss of sound in the first debate led Lionel Van Deerlin, the chairman of the House Subcommittee on Communications, to state that the event had "made a mockery" of the FCC interpretation of Section 315.[13] "The networks knew what they were talking about in the first place," he said, "as long as candidates are going to be hermetically sealed anyway, they should have been where they belong in the first place—in a studio."[14] Even the League's project director, James Karayn, remarked that the whole matter was similar to "going to the ball park through the opening in the fence, rather than through the door."[15] Eugene McCarthy, the independent candidate who was challenging the FCC's interpretation of Section 315, argued that stopping the first debate when the television broadcast was interrupted proved his claim that the debates were controlled by the networks and were not a "bona fide news event." The FCC rejected this argument, observing that the League, not the networks, had made the decision to stop the debate when the interruption occurred.[16]

A debate organized by the networks would require, under present law and FCC regulations, that the networks provide "equal opportunities" nationwide to all minor party and independent candidates who had qualified for a place on the presidential ballot (or who made substantial showing[17] of being a write-in candidate) in ten or more states. Even candidates on the ballot in only a single state would have to be accorded "equal opportunities" by broadcast stations serving the state. In 1960, for example, were it not for the suspension of Section 315, many hours of broadcast time would have been made available to some or all of the more than fifteen other candidates, including the American Beat Consensus candidate, the Tax Cut party candidate, and Homer Tomlison, self-proclaimed "King of the World."[18]

Section 315 could, of course, be amended by Congress to exempt debates, including those organized by the networks, from the "equal time" requirement. Alternatively, Congress might choose to repeal the provision entirely, as broadcasters have requested for years, or at least suspend it for presidential elections as was done in 1960. Other possibilities would include a revision of the section to make sure that only truly significant candidates became entitled to "equal time" or any time as a result of the broadcast of a debate between other significant candidates. This would, of course, require the development of criteria to distinguish the significant candidate from those who have no important role in the election (see Chapter VII).

Because presidential debates are a political event and are part of the electoral process, responsibility for them might be given to the political parties—the Republican and Democratic National Committees. The parties already are responsible for the development of platforms setting out the policies of their candidates; by providing advice, personnel, and funds, the national parties already attempt to facilitate the presentation of the candidates to the public. Responsibility for the debates would not be inconsistent, therefore, with the parties' present role. Looking to the political parties to provide the impetus for and organization of debates might be a means of revitalizing the party function. Recent years have witnessed a decline in the role of the parties, a decline caused at least in part by television taking the place of the local party worker in familiarizing the voter with the party's candidate. This decline has diminished the importance of the platform in elections, lessened opportunities for citizen participation in the electoral process, and threatened the political balances that have allowed Congress to legislate with any semblance of coherence. Responsibility for televised presidential debates would give the parties a new long-term function integral to the new medium of politics.

The parties' interest in the debates, however, may be based on the degree to which they believe a debate would improve the chances of their own candidate. The parties are "win-lose" oriented and not necessarily interested in improving public knowledge—unless doing so will help their candidate win. Without a legal requirement that a candidate participate in debates (see Chapter VI), party-organized debates will take place only when both candidates are readily willing to debate, and that has happened only twice in the more than a quarter of a century since television emerged as a political medium.

Moreover, while it is true that candidates had a major role in choosing debate formats and issues in 1960 and 1976, the networks and the League of Women Voters, respectively, did at least have some effect on format decisions in those years. If the debates were controlled by the parties, the candidates would have a free hand in determining the format and issues, and their decisions on these matters are likely to be motivated largely by what they think would be best for their candidacy rather than what information would be most helpful to the public in making an informed decision.

A third possibility for the allocation of responsibility for the debates is public service or educational organizations, most obviously the League of Women Voters, which now has the experience of 1976 to add to a long and unique history of voter education activities. The encouragement and organization of presidential debates in the future is likely to be of interest not only to the League but also to journalism fraternities, policy research institutions, and scholarly associations. Many of these groups also could satisfy the FCC's requirement that the debates, to be free of the "equal time" obligation when broadcast, be organized by an entity not associated with the broadcasters.

Placing responsibility for the debates with a public service or educational organization has the advantage of giving the assignment to a group that is already in a good position to deal with the sometimes conflicting demands of and among candidates and broadcasters, thus lessening the possibility that disagreements would interfere with the attainment of debate goals. The nonpartisanship of the proper organization would help ensure the absence of bias and enhance the credibility of the events. The proper group also can add prestige to the events, as the League did in 1976. A service or educational organization, free of the economic pressures that affect the networks and of the political pressures affecting the parties, would be in the best position to speak for the public's interest in the debates.

Although relations between the League of Women Voters and the networks often seemed strained during the planning for the 1976 debates, even the network representative most upset at the League during those sessions, Richard Salant of CBS News, later acknowledged that the League did substantially as well as the networks themselves could have done:

> In respect of format or other basic arrangements, I am not at all sure that we—the network news organizations—could have done significantly better than the League. *Perhaps* we might have been a little more sophisticated. *Perhaps* we would have bargained a little harder. *Perhaps* the set would have looked a little less like the village thermometer showing how well the local United Fund drive was doing. *Perhaps* we would not have given in to some of the candidates' demands so quickly because at least in some respects the networks might have had a little more clout (even that is arguable since it may well be that Presidential candidates might find it more difficult to disagree with, and pull out of an event under the auspices of, so prestigious, unassailable and formidable a public service organization as the League of Women Voters than one under the auspices of the mean, male-dominated, big old networks).
>
> But, I find nothing wrong with the mere fact of having such events under the auspices of a responsible outside organization, nor do the networks have any God-given right to be the only ones to arrange such events.[19]

Moreover, placing responsibility for debates with a public service or educational organization could allow interested citizens groups to take part in the debates and in this way to be active in the electoral process. The League of Women Voters, for example, has almost 150,000 active members in almost 1,400 state and local leagues throughout the country. The debates need not even be the responsibility of a single public service or educational organization; they could be the joint undertaking of a variety of groups, perhaps with disparate backgrounds or memberships. The groups could form a steering committee or council to organize the debates under the sponsors' direction. Placing the responsibility for debates in the hands of these groups, therefore, could give the broad public a greater role in what is, after all, a public responsibility.

The arguments against giving control of the debates to public service groups include the issue of journalistic control referred to earlier—the position of the networks that control of the coverage of "news events" should rest with the media. In addition, like the networks, public service groups would not be readily subject to any form of compulsion, and if no organization stepped forward voluntarily, or if the organization performed badly, the debates might not be held or might be held in such a way as to be less useful. The participation of private organizations also may raise more difficult problems with respect to financing the debates (see Chapter V).

The final possibility for assigning responsibility for the debates is the federal government. James Karayn has suggested, for example, the establishment of a National Debate Commission, whose commissioners would be selected from civic and political groups, the broadcast industry, business, unions, and persons familiar with the issues likely to arise in a debate. The commission would establish the schedule and format for debates, provide guidelines for candidates and broadcasters, and attempt to kindle public interest.[20]

A *Washington Star* editorial shortly after the 1976 debates suggested that "perhaps debates should be . . . arranged, say, by the Federal Election Commission or some other appropriate [government] unit."[21] The Federal Election Commission (FEC) was established in 1974 to administer and enforce federal campaign disclosure requirements, contribution and expenditure limitations, and the public financing of presidential primaries and elections. The FEC is composed of the Secretary of the Senate and the Clerk of the House (*ex officio* without the right to vote) and six members appointed by the president and confirmed by the Senate.[22]

The argument in favor of this proposal is that a government entity would assure permanence since, presumably, the entity would have an obligation under law to perform its responsibilities and could not pursue debates only in those years when it had some political motivation to do so. On the other hand, debates organized by a Federal Debate Commission or the FEC could lead to even more friction between the broadcast press and the debate organizer than occurred in 1976. As long as all candidates are not included in debate projects, moreover, government participation will raise constitutional issues that, although probably not sufficient to prevent the effectuation of such a plan, are significant enough to surround it with lengthy litigation (see Chapter V). And as Associated Press correspondent Walter Mears has commented:

> No doubt, government could stage . . . the debates directly. . . . But the greater the government role, the more the process becomes subject to the interests of the party in power, in Congress and the White House.[23]

V/Financing Televised Debates*

The 1976 debates cost the League of Women Voters more than $325,000 in expenses and the broadcast networks about $6 million in lost revenues. While these costs may be only a small part of the many more millions of dollars spent on a presidential election, they can be a substantial burden for a potential debate sponsor.

As the 1976 figures indicate, the actual organization of the debates, including the sponsor's extra staff, rental of the hall (if any), construction of sets, transportation and lodging for the moderator and panelists (if any), accommodations for the media, and a variety of operational expenses, can be expected to be less expensive than the value of the time used to broadcast the events. Nevertheless, preparations can become costly. In 1960, the network sponsors spared no expense in planning the debates, constructing special sets and providing top personnel. They furnished elaborate accommodations for the candidates, even, for the final debates, building identical cottages in the network studio for the use of each candidate:

> After several plans, ranging from "vine-covered honeymoon" to "contemporary-simple," a modified colonial exterior was adopted. They [the cottages] were air conditioned and each had two rooms, one of which included a lavatory. . . . The cottages' exteriors were completely finished.[1]

The television time devoted to the broadcast of the debates can be expected to continue to be expensive; the $6 million in lost network revenues in 1976 was a substantial increase over the $2.5 million lost in

---

*Susan Tifft of Washington, D.C., assisted in the preparation of this chapter.

1960.[2] Moreover, television coverage by all of the networks involves other costs as well, including employee time, equipment rental, transportation, and lodging. This coverage is essential, however, for the impact of televised presidential debates is largely attributable to the audiences the debates have reached, and these audiences have resulted from the networks' willingness to broadcast the debates simultaneously in "prime time" viewing hours.

The question of who can or should pay the cost of organizing and broadcasting debates in the future requires an examination of the Federal Election Campaign Act and rules and policies of the FEC. The act requires that federal candidates and political committees report the source and extent of the contributions they receive and the expenditures they make. The act limits the amount that an individual may contribute to candidates or political committees to a nominal sum, and prohibits *any* contribution "in connection with . . . any [federal] election" by corporations and unions.

The Campaign Act also established a Presidential Election Campaign Fund raised by voluntary, one-dollar donations authorized by individual taxpayers, who simply check a box on their federal tax returns if they wish to contribute. The FEC distributes this money to qualified presidential candidates for use in their primary and general election campaigns; the political parties also receive an allocation for their conventions. Candidates who accept this federal funding for their campaign, however, may accept no campaign contributions from other sources. All of these provisions are administered by the FEC, but any rules adopted by the commission may be vetoed by the House or the Senate.

The costs of future debates, like the responsibility for organizing them, might be borne by the networks, public service or educational groups, the political parties, or the government.

The networks paid the full cost of the 1960 debates and bore the cost of televising the 1976 debates, including the cost of the television time. As discussed in the preceding chapter, the networks have indicated a strong desire to play the same role they played in 1960 in the future, presumably including not only the donation of television time but also the payment of the cost of organizing the debates if they are to have that responsibility. While the possibility of allocating responsibility for future debates to the networks raised a number of questions discussed earlier, the prospect of continued network donation of television time and payment of their own costs of coverage promises to be a benefit without any readily identifiable disadvantage. The networks are providing the time because they hope to benefit indirectly and over the long term, but that is of no particular concern. Under these circumstances, it appears desirable that this network role continue, regardless of what determination is made about whether the networks should organize the debates.[3]

The more difficult question is whether the networks should be compelled to provide free time if they no longer wish to provide it. That is, if a private party, a political party, or the government were to control the debates, should the networks be required to provide free time for them?

As noted earlier, by reason of their use of the limited public airwaves, broadcasters function as trustees of the channels on which they operate and may be compelled to perform in a manner reasonably deemed by Congress or the FCC to be in the public interest. The "equal time" provision is founded on this concept, as is the requirement that reasonable access to broadcast time be provided to federal candidates. If the televising of debates were found to be sufficiently important, and if it appeared unlikely that they could be assured in other ways, Congress might seek to require the broadcasters to provide free time for presidential debates.

On the other hand, while the courts have been more concerned with the First Amendment right of the public to receive news and information than they have with the rights of broadcasters, it is by no means clear that Congress could dictate carriage of a particular program. Even if legally permissible, compelling time for one event could lead to growing pressures to compel the provision of time for other events (for example, appearances by members of Congress), to a point where a substantial part of broadcast content could become determined by government fiat. Finally, the cost of the television time used for the debates is quite substantial, and it may not be appropriate to tax only the broadcast industry to provide a service that benefits all segments of the national interest.

The networks might be encouraged to cover the debates if they were compensated for the time. For example, in 1969, the Twentieth Century Fund Commission on Campaign Costs in the Electronic Era proposed that broadcasters provide time (called "voters' time") for presidential candidates to appear on all broadcast stations simultaneously.[4] Under this proposal, broadcasters would be required to provide the time but would be paid for it by the government at one-half the broadcasters' usual rates or the lowest rate charged a commercial advertiser, whichever was lower. The commission concluded that this arrangement satisfied the objective of having the public pay for what was, after all, a public benefit, while at the same time ensuring that private interests would not profit. Applying this principle to presidential debates would mean that the networks would receive payment for debate time, but not at their full rates.

Broadcasters could also be compensated through changes in the tax laws that would provide tax advantages for the donation of television time for presidential debates and, perhaps, other election programming. This would not only compensate the networks for the time provided but also might encourage many stations to carry election programming not carried by the networks. A similar approach has been suggested by a Campaign Study Group formed by the Institute of Politics at Harvard University. The group has recommended that "networks and licensees should be permitted to deduct full costs of production and lost advertising revenues for [public service] programming offered during prime . . . time (7:30–11:00 p.m.) and two-thirds of costs during other program time." Presidential debates would appear to be a form of public service programming entitling broadcasters to deductions under such a tax incentive program.[5]

If the networks are to be paid for use of their time (in a form other than tax incentives), payment must come from one or more of the remaining parties under consideration—public service or educational organizations, the political parties, or the government. Moreover, unless the organization of debates is made a network responsibility, organization costs would have to be paid out of one of these pockets.

The efforts of the League of Women Voters to fund televised presidential debates in 1976 demonstrated the difficulty of depending on private sector financing for this purpose under present law and policy. Both Jimmy Carter and Gerald Ford elected to take full public funding for their general election efforts in 1976, the first election year for which this option was available under the Campaign Act. This meant that each candidate received $21.8 million in government funds for the general election campaign, with the condition that the candidate accept no outside contributions during that campaign. The law defines a contribution for this purpose as a "gift, subscription, loan, advance, or deposit of money or anything of value made for the purpose of . . . influencing . . . the election of any person to Federal office."[6] This definition was the focal point of arguments in 1976 concerning the permissible role of the League or any other private party in financing television debates.

When the League announced that its Education Fund would sponsor the Carter-Ford debates, the question arose as to whether the League's sponsorship was a "contribution" as defined in the law and, therefore, prohibited in a general election contest in which neither candidate could accept private contributions. Would the debates "influence" the election in a way the law intended to restrict? Did the fact that the debates would not include all presidential candidates (there were over 100 candidates registered with the FEC at the time) mean that League sponsorship had to be viewed as "influencing" the election of the major party candidates in preference to the other candidates?

Still another question in 1976 was whether the League could use donations from corporations or unions to pay for the debates. As noted above, the law prohibits corporations and unions from making contributions "in connection with . . . an election." While contributions to a debate project appeared to be "in connection with" an election, the League believed its nonpartisan history and its avowed purpose in staging the debates—to provide information to the electorate and to educate voters—should take the contribution out of the prohibited category.

Within days of the League's announcement that it would fund the debates, the FEC began to examine these questions.[7] The issue of the use of corporate and union donations to fund candidate debates had first arisen in the fall of 1975, when the League asked for and received an informal opinion from the FEC concerning the League's sponsorship of the Presidential Forums. The League had asked the FEC to decide whether corporate gifts to help defray the cost of holding the forums would be considered prohibited contributions. In its request for a ruling, the League chronicled its long history of nonpartisan involvement in elections and voter education and cited the Education Fund's designation as a "501 (c) (3)" organization under the Internal Revenue Code—that is, an organization that did not participate in campaigns on behalf of particular candidates for public office. The League argued that since the Education Fund was truly nonpartisan, both for legal purposes and in practice, corporate contributions to it for use in the forums were for educational rather than for partisan purposes and, consequently, were lawful.

In an opinion by its general counsel, the FEC agreed with the League's interpretation but added a caveat. The opinion stated that corporate contributions to the Education Fund would be legal "provided the Fund's activities do not have the effect of supporting or favoring particular parties or candidates." Apparently, this meant that the fund should include independent candidates (for example, Eugene McCarthy) in the forums to demonstrate that particular parties or candidates were not being favored:

> It is my opinion . . . that from time to time the League should seek to include such other persons who, while not qualified for a primary ballot because of their independent status, are nonetheless individuals of such national stature that their inclusion in the Forums will maximize their educational benefit to the public.[8]

The League, taking this more as a suggestion than a requirement, invited only those candidates who had qualified for public funding in the primary elections,[9] which excluded independent and minor party candidates. Since the FEC did not challenge the League's action, it ap-

peared that the League had established the principle that it could
finance debates from corporate and union sources even if independent
candidates were not included.

The legality of League sponsorship of debates had not been directly
at issue during the forums because neither the League nor the FEC apparently gave any thought to the possibility that League payments
could be considered to be "for the purpose of . . . influencing" the
election. In fact, by emphasizing that all of the primary candidates
would be invited to debate and the educational benefits of the forums,
the FEC general counsel's opinion on corporate contributions assumed
that the League sponsorship would not be for the purpose of influencing the election. In the general election, however, the League found
that not only was its use of corporate and union funds at issue again but
also that there was a possibility that its sponsorship of the Carter-Ford
debates would be found to constitute an unlawful contribution.

Suggestions that the FEC might prohibit the League from presenting
the presidential debates brought a surge of disapproval from the press
and public. The *Washington Star,* for example, advised the FEC to
"call off its bureaucratic dogs."[10] The League, meanwhile, pointed out
that if the FEC were to declare its sponsorship of the debates an illegal
contribution the action would "fundamentally alter the electoral process" because it would have the effect of labeling as illegal many pri-
vately sponsored events in which presidential candidates had appeared
for years, including speeches to civic and educational groups, church
picnics, and National Press Club forums.[11]

The FEC decided not to bar the League's sponsorship of the 1976
debates, but it did seriously restrict the League's ability to finance the
events. The commission held that, due to the nonpartisan nature of the
League, its sponsorship of the debates was not "for the purpose of
influencing" an election and, therefore, was not an illegal "contribution":

> The League has a history of approximately 50 years of nonpartisan educa-
> tional activity in the electoral process, and is, indeed, forbidden by its by-
> laws to endorse candidates or to otherwise appear in a partisan light. The
> activity proposed to be undertaken here is in keeping with that tradition.
> Unlike sponsorship of an appearance by a single candidate, the unavoidable
> impact of which is to advance the chances of that candidate's election, the
> debate described in the League's proposal does not involve that kind of ad-
> vocacy or assistance to a campaign to which [the law's] contribution limits
> are directed. In short, it is the Commission's view that the disbursements by
> the League, or by any other comparable or similarly qualified organization,
> through a charitable trust fund, are not made for the purpose of influencing a
> Federal election and are therefore not contributions as defined in [the law].[12]

The commission, however, decided that the League could not accept corporate or union money (including donations from incorporated foundations) to help defray its costs. The FEC reasoned that contributions to the debates were undeniably "in connection with" an election and, therefore, within the definition of a prohibited contribution when made by corporations or unions; it made no attempt to reconcile this decision with its earlier decision that corporate contributions could be used to support the candidate forums during the primary elections.

League President Ruth Clausen later testified that the FEC's barring of corporate, union, and foundation donations had a "devastating effect on the Education Fund's plans to fund [the debates]."[13] The decision caused the League financial difficulty; the Education Fund paid more than $325,000 in debate bills, but since it had raised only about $225,000 in private contributions, the $100,000 deficit had to be made up from the League's own treasury. The League referred to its FEC problems in a quarter-page advertisement in the *Washington Post* in September 1976:

YOU CAN HELP 1976 PRESIDENTIAL DEBATES

The League of Women Voters had planned to fund these debates through a variety of sources, but the Federal Election Commission has ruled to the contrary. As a result, we are launching a public appeal to individuals to help us meet the costs of these historic events.[14]

The League sought reversal of the FEC decision in the courts. The FEC decision also was appealed by Eugene McCarthy and the American party, both of whom alleged that the League's support was illegal because it discriminated against independent and third-party candidates. A federal court dismissed both cases without opinion. After holding hearings of its own in 1977, however, the FEC reversed itself again, concluding:

A corporation or labor organization may donate funds for use in the sponsorship of nonpartisan public debates if the donation is made to a nonprofit organization which is exempt from federal taxation under 26 U.S.C. §501 (c) (3), which has a history of neither supporting nor endorsing candidates or political parties, and which administers the fund.[15]

Although this position was reached more than a year ago, the FEC has not incorporated it into a regulation for submission to Congress, which has veto power over new FEC rules.

Although the dust may not yet have fully settled over the 1976 controversies, it presently appears lawful for private organizations with a

history of nonpartisan activity to fund future presidential debates—
that is, as long as they obtain their own funds from individual contribu-
tors. Assuming that the most recent FEC position is placed in a rule
and not vetoed by Congress, an organization may utilize corporate and
union funds if it is a "501 (c) (3)" organization, which includes the
League's Education Fund and

> corporations, and any community chest, fund, or foundation, organized
> and operated exclusively for religious, charitable, scientific . . . literary,
> or educational purposes . . . no part of the net earnings of which inures to
> the benefit of any private shareholder or individual, no substantial part of
> the activities of which is carrying on propaganda, or otherwise attempting to
> influence legislation . . . and which does not participate in, or intervene in
> (including the publishing or distributing of statements), any political cam-
> paign on behalf of any candidate for public office.[16]

Because the FEC's rulings on all of the debate issues have not clearly
explained the commission's reasoning, however, some uncertainty remains.

If the decision is that debate expenses (organizational cost, television time cost, or both) should be left to the generosity of private organizations, Congress and the FEC could make it easier for the organizations to fund the debates by making it clear that the contribution pro-
hibitions are not applicable to either the payment of debate costs or to
donations to the project by corporations or unions. It may be that the
most important test is that of nonpartisanship and that any organization able to demonstrate nonpartisanship and independence from control by any partisan entity should be able to fund debates regardless of
the source of its funds.

Using political party funds to pay for televised presidential debates
also would raise questions under the campaign laws. The national committees of the Democratic and Republican parties are permitted, within
certain limits, to raise funds and to make expenditures on behalf of the
parties' candidates. But the question of whether an expenditure for debates would be treated as coming in place of or in addition to the
spending limitations applicable to the parties would have to be answered. Moreover, changes in the laws and regulations would be required if it were determined that the parties are to use corporate and
union donations for the purpose of funding debates.

Relying on the political parties to fund debates would mean relying
not only on their willingness to do so but also on their ability to find the
financial resources to pay for debates. It also would mean relying on
their ability to agree between themselves on the sharing of expenses.
Fund-raising difficulties or disagreements between the parties could
prevent the debates from taking place.

As indicated above, 1976 was the first general election year paid for by the federal government. It would be a natural extension of this concept, and of the present use of the "check off" fund, to pay for future presidential debates in the same manner, regardless of where the responsibility for organizing the events had been allocated.

If the networks are given responsibility for future debates, they could be reimbursed by the government in a manner similar to the "voters' time" funding proposal discussed above. Reimbursement could come directly from the government or from the candidates, who would be given funds specifically for this purpose.

Similarly, if a private party, such as the League, were to have responsibility for future debates, that party could receive government grants for this purpose. The government might even solicit proposals from various groups wishing to organize the debates and able to meet nonpartisanship criteria established by the FEC or by Karayn's proposed National Debate Commission. The FEC or the Debate Commission could provide "seed money" to the most promising of these groups to undertake the initial organization of the debates and, if the debates then materialize, could fund the remaining expenses by further grants.

If the political parties were to have responsibility for future debates, they, too, could be the recipients of federal funding earmarked for this purpose. Finally, if the government itself were given responsibility for future debates, funding could be part of the budget of the FEC, a Debate Commission, or any existing or new agency that Congress set up to perform this role.

The federal payment for future presidential televised debates might come most logically from the Presidential Election Campaign Fund. This would ensure that the events are paid for by those most interested in them. Since the debates clearly serve a public function that benefits the entire populace, however, it would not seem inappropriate to fund them through general tax revenues if the Campaign Fund became overburdened. Even if neither of these methods were deemed acceptable, the government might at least authorize the FEC, a Debate Commission, or some other agency to receive donations from individuals, corporations, unions, and virtually any other source; the agency would then disburse these funds to pay for debates in one of the ways discussed above.

Government funding of the presidential debates again raises concern about governmental intrusion and control. Moreover, discrimination against minor party candidates and independent candidates, in the form of exclusion from the debates, would be subject to challenge if the debates were funded by the government. While a system of federal funding may be sustained by the courts, litigation could leave the matter in doubt for some time.

The Supreme Court has upheld the present system of using public funds to finance presidential campaigns even though the system makes a clear distinction between major party candidates and other candidates. The Court held that financial assistance could be limited to candidates with substantial electoral support without violating constitutional principles:

> The denial of public financing to some presidential candidates is not restrictive of voters' rights and less restrictive of candidates'. The statute does not prevent any candidate from getting on the ballot or any voter from casting a ballot for the candidate of his choice; the inability, if any, of minority-party candidates to wage effective campaigns will derive not from lack of public funding but from their inability to raise private contributions.[17]

Consequently, it is likely that a system of federal funding for presidential debates would be sustained even if participation in the debates generally was limited to the Democratic and Republican candidates.

The constitutionality of federal funding of debates that exclude minor party candidates, however, is not free from doubt. The challengers are likely to argue that, even if federal grants of money to major party candidates do not restrict the minor parties in their campaigning, the grant of television time only to the major parties creates just such a restriction. It uses scarce broadcast time that might otherwise be available to the minor parties, and more importantly, it assures the major candidates access to the most effective means of convincing the public not to support minor party candidates. It might also be argued that the federal campaign funding system approved by the courts differs from funding of debates in that the former does make full funding available to the candidates of any party that received at least 25 percent of the popular vote in the last presidential election, makes some funding available to candidates of parties that received between 5 and 25 percent of the vote in the last election, and reimburses all other candidates for part of their expenses if they receive 5 percent of the votes in the election. In contrast, the debates might have more stringent requirements for inclusion or might not provide for any debate participation at all by minor parties.

Despite these problems, government funding of future presidential televised debates offers one substantial advantage that most of the other alternatives do not offer. Unlike private organizations and political party committees, the government can be counted on to have the funds available to pay for the debates. Debate expenditures would constitute but a small portion of the campaign payments made by the government to the candidates.

VI/Candidate Participation in Televised Debates

Presidential debates have had an erratic history largely because presidential candidates have been reluctant to participate unless they believed the events would be to their advantage. Debates have occurred only when *both* candidates, almost by historical accident, concluded that participation would either gain them votes or prevent the loss of votes. Determining who should bear the responsibility for televised presidential debates and who should bear their costs, therefore, does not necessarily ensure that the candidates will participate.

It has been said that "one of the oldest axioms of American politics is that well-known candidates should not appear jointly with or in any other way lend their prestige to lesser-known opponents."[1] The same axiom has been applied to the "favorite" candidate. Joe Napolitan, an experienced media advisor to politicians, once commented, "If I had a candidate who was a clear favorite, I'd try to keep him off TV debates."[2] It is similarly axiomatic that an incumbent candidate has little incentive to appear with an opponent in a televised debate or anything else. As a result, where one candidate for president is well-known and the other is not, where one candidate is an incumbent, or where one candidate is heavily favored, joint appearances, including debates, will be avoided by one candidate to the extent possible.[3]

The experience in the forums during the 1976 primaries supports this hypothesis. When invitations to the first forum were issued in the early stages of the primaries, the invitations were accepted quickly by the underdogs—Fred Harris, Milton Shapp, Jimmy Carter, and Sargent Shriver; Senator Henry Jackson, the Democratic front-runner, agreed to participate only at the last minute and after considerable cajoling. As Jimmy Carter began to win primaries, it became progressively more difficult to convince him to participate in the remaining forums; by the fourth forum in Chicago, he already had beaten Jackson in Pennsylvania and declined to appear.

71

There are many other examples of the hesitancy or refusal of better known, favored, or incumbent candidates to engage in debate with opponents. Even Stephen Douglas recognized before his first debate with Lincoln that, as the better known of the two and the favorite, he had little to gain. "If he gets the best of this debate . . . I shall lose everything. Should I win, I shall gain but little."[4] More than a century later, with the 1960 Kennedy-Nixon debates fresh in mind, then retired President Eisenhower observed that "if I were giving one political piece of advice . . . I would say, 'When you're in, never debate with an outer.' "[5] This advice was taken to heart by Lyndon Johnson, the incumbent and favorite in 1964. As Robert MacNeil has written, "inviting Senator Goldwater into the same TV studio with President Johnson would have been to haul him back from the outer reaches of that extremist wasteland to which the Democrats had consigned him."[6]

It is not only the incumbent or leading candidate who is not eager to confront an opposing candidate in a debate. A lesser known challenger may believe, for example, that the incumbent's word would carry greater weight in a debate, particularly in times of national crisis, or that the incumbent has better access to the media to explain and to qualify what is said in a debate. An inexperienced candidate also may fear being unduly aggressive beside a distinguished opponent. Many candidates may worry that their television "image" will not be so attractive as that of their opponent. Finally, a candidate simply may not wish to risk being attacked in a vulnerable area before an audience of millions; for example, in 1968 both Hubert Humphrey and Richard Nixon chose not to risk an inquiry into their Vietnam peace plans.

In general, however, the candidate who is not an incumbent, is lesser known, or is believed to be an underdog will wish to debate since he has little to lose and much to gain. One political advisor has counseled, for example:

> It is always possible that a witty remark, a pointed barb, a flurry of statistics, or a startling revelation can turn the tide or that the front runner may "blow the election" . . . by "being stupid, impolite, or who the hell knows what." Televised debates not only present the underdog with a unique opportunity to get in a crippling blow but also provide him with badly needed free time and equal exposure. Professional politicians agree, therefore, that it is wise for the candidate who is behind to debate unless he is hopelessly inept, stupid, or physically repulsive.[7]

In any event, a candidate's decision about whether to debate inevitably is largely political. "The rational candidate," concludes one observer of candidate debates, "makes strategic decisions in terms of political expediency not civic duty."[8]

A "textbook" example of the political nature of the decision to debate or not to debate was the 1962 Massachusetts senatorial contest between Edward Kennedy and Edward McCormack. In the primary, both candidates agreed to televised debates because each saw them to be to his particular advantage. McCormack's advisors believed the debates would be a way of exposing Kennedy as brash, too young, simply trading on the family name, and prone to irrational temper:

> [I]n a debate with Ted Kennedy, Ed McCormack can light Mr. Kennedy's extremely short fuse. I think this [Kennedy] is a guy who could blow it on television. Ted Kennedy could be angered to the point where he could make a public display of his very famous temper. . . . This would be highly injurious and accrue to our benefit.[9]

On the other hand, Kennedy saw the debates as an opportunity to show that he was vigorous, articulate, and a more attractive candidate than McCormack. Kennedy's advisors noted that "he talks like a Kennedy . . . he's got vigor . . . he's an excellent and articulate person, and he makes a very strong presentation." They saw McCormack, in contrast, as having "kind of a bad smile . . . and a little bit of lisp . . . and he doesn't come through quite as well on television as he does in person." [10]

In the primary election debates, McCormack claimed Kennedy offered the voters nothing but a famous name and suggested the Kennedy candidacy would be hopeless if his name were simply Edward Moore instead of Edward Moore Kennedy. Interestingly, the attack inspired an outpouring of sympathy for Kennedy and hostility to McCormack that seemed to help Kennedy in the primary. Taking no further chances, however, Kennedy refused to debate his Republican and independent opponents in the general election, leaving them to hold a televised debate with an empty chair.[11]

There is one circumstance in which a decision by a candidate, and particularly an incumbent candidate, not to debate may be founded on other than essentially political considerations. An incumbent president may determine in good faith that the debate or discussion of an important current issue could have an adverse impact on national diplomacy or world affairs. Shortly after the 1960 debates, *The New Republic* questioned the wisdom and propriety of "a Chief Magistrate and the policies, the secrets, and the prestige of his regime [being] made targets of direct, unrehearsed partisan interpretation—perhaps at a dangerous moment of world affairs."[12] Similarly, the 1964 Report of the American Political Science Association Commission studying debates concluded that whether debates should be held was "less certain when one of the . . . candidates is President" since "extraordinary situations may be created by the exigencies of the world situation and the international position of the U.S. In some of these situations it may be contrary to our national interest for the President to engage in debates.''13

While an unusual international or even domestic situation might make it improper or dangerous for an incumbent to comment on a particular matter, there would seem to be no reason why a debate could not be held and confined to other matters by agreement among the candidates or with the debate organizer. The challenger probably would prefer this to no debate at all and would not, in any event, wish to appear insensitive to a national crisis or to the need for diplomatic delicacy.

When candidates wish to avoid televised debates for any reason, they have not hesitated to take evasive measures. Joe Napolitan has suggested how this can be done:

> . . . I would never openly refuse to debate. If challenged to a debate, you say, "Yes, sure. How about my campaign manager meeting yours at 4 p.m. on Thursday?" Then five to four on Thursday, you call and say, "We've had a real crisis here, can we make it on Saturday?" And on Saturday you put it off till next Wednesday . . . and so on.14

A candidate who does not wish to debate can observe loftily that debates "would serve no useful purpose," belittle the affair as a media event with no meaning, or, if an incumbent, argue that sensitive international relationships could be jeopardized. For example, when Gerald Ford refused to debate Ronald Reagan during the 1976 Republican primary, Ford's campaign staff claimed that he had done so because the debate would be only "a test of who is the best showman, and . . . it's degrading to the office of the Presidency."15

Other candidates, such as Edward Kennedy in 1962, have allowed their opponents to debate without them. In that same year, in the Pennsylvania gubernatorial campaign, William Scranton refused to debate Richard Dilworth on television, but when Dilworth staged a debate with an empty chair, Scranton showed up at the studio with a bucket of whitewash and accused Dilworth of trying to smear him.16 In the 1974 New York senatorial campaign, Robert Kennedy ducked a televised debate with Kenneth Keating; when Keating tried the empty chair technique, Kennedy appeared at the studio and demanded to participate, probably knowing that he would not be allowed in at the last minute but that he could use the publicity to cloud the issue of who had refused to debate whom.17

The two presidential debates to date have taken place because neither candidate was an elected incumbent or heavily favored, and because both believed it in their interest to participate. In 1960, Richard

Nixon said, "I was better known than he [Kennedy] and our joint appearance would simply build up an audience for him,"[18] but Nixon also believed that there was good reason to think the debates would help him beat Kennedy. Nixon had been a success in college debating; he had debated successfully with his opponent in his first campaign for election to Congress; he had enhanced his career in 1959 by the "Kitchen Debate" with Soviet Premier Khrushchev at an industrial exhibition in Moscow; he had developed a public image as a "fighter" when vice-president by standing up to hostile crowds during state visits to South America; and he had used television with great success in his famous "Checkers" speech defending himself against slush fund charges in the 1952 campaign.

Nixon also probably recognized that the debate would increase his exposure among Democrats, who outnumbered Republicans by a large margin, some of whom he would have to convert if he were to win. He also believed that by appearing on television as "a fine fellow who reeks of sincerity,"[19] he could counter the "Tricky Dick" image that had plagued him. Finally, he believed that, "Had I refused the challenge, I would have opened myself to the charge that I was afraid to stand on our [the Eisenhower administration] record."[20]

Kennedy similarly evaluated the debates in terms of their potential impact on his election. He, too, believed himself a good debater, having successfully debated his 1952 senatorial opponent, Hubert Humphrey in the West Virginia primary, and Lyndon Johnson at the Democratic convention. He believed that he could project a good television image and that the debates would make him better known and help him counter an image of inexperience and immaturity.[21]

In 1976, candidates Ford and Carter also conducted a political analysis to determine whether they should debate. The Ford situation was particularly unique. Although he was the incumbent president and had been vice-president before that, he had never run for national office. As a result, he had no political organization in place to solicit support in the traditional grass-roots manner. Because Ford had had to campaign heavily in the primaries against Ronald Reagan, he also lacked the usual nonpolitical image of a presidential incumbent. Moreover, the Republican convention had come late, leaving Ford less time than his opponent to campaign; and since both candidates were receiving equal federal funds for their campaigns, Ford had no more money to spend on his campaign to make up for the lost time. Finally, although his opponent was far ahead in the polls, Ford believed Carter's support was "soft" and was based on an unclear or inaccurate idea of what he stood for; the more Carter could be forced to take specific positions on issues, the more he would lose support. Ford's aides summarized their analysis this way:

[W]e . . . believed that debates showing our opponent and the President
responding to specific questions about their views on substantive issues
would play to our strengths and to Governor Carter's weaknesses, and
might convince a number of voters that they disagreed with him in certain
areas. . . .

*   *   *

More importantly, the debates . . . satisfied our need to mount an aggressive, come-from-behind campaign, and provided a justification for staying
off the campaign trail as much as possible. Finally, our unconventional circumstances called for an unconventional response. We had few alternatives.[22]

In deciding whether or not he should debate, Jimmy Carter took into
consideration his ability to outscore his opponent on television. If Ronald Reagan were the candidate, he concluded that he probably would
not debate. He recognized that Reagan "was a superb user of the television media [and] I would have been at a disadvantage then."[23] With
Ford as the nominee, however, Carter knew that he would not be up
against a television professional. His advisors also noted that, since
there were no "burning issues" in the campaign, voters were likely to
decide their votes on the basis of their perception of the candidates.
Since there were more Democrats than Republicans, and since the
polls showed them leaning toward Carter, his advisors reasoned that
debates could solidify that vote:

We had to debate to reinforce those people who intended to vote for Carter.
Debates would give him depth exposure, would demonstrate his compe-
tence in the same arena with an incumbent president, would retain his solid
vote—and keep reinforcing it. . . . In other words, people leaning for
Carter watched the debates wanting to be assured the candidate was not
some latter-day Rasputin but rather exuded that kind of calm confidence
and knowledge that would merit the vote they planned to give him.[24]

The history of debates, including attempts at debates, suggests that,
as Jimmy Carter's advisors observed after the most recent debates,
"although pressure to debate will be greater than ever on future presidential candidates, the decision to have them . . . will remain political decisions which will differ from campaign to campaign."[25] Candidate participation in future debates could, of course, simply be left to
chance and to these political decisions. In the words of one commentator, " [W]e can wait for another coincidence. All it takes is an incumbent president who is thirty-three points behind in the polls, and an opponent who nevertheless figures he may have a recognition problem."[26]
On the other hand, the better policy may be to seek methods of assuring that future candidates will debate.

The purpose of a candidate's election campaign, of course, is to create a public perception of a candidate as more qualified than his opponent to hold the office in question. One way of influencing a candidate's decision about television debates, therefore, is to increase the importance of that decision in the public perception of the candidate's qualifications. Public pressure, in other words, could force a candidate to debate if his refusal could be shown to have an important negative impact on public opinion about him.

The public does want televised presidential debates: a nationwide postelection poll in 1976 found that 66 percent of those polled want the 1980 presidential candidates to participate in televised debates.[27] The League of Women Voters believed it could obtain millions of signatures in a petition drive seeking support for the 1976 debates. Possibly, the public recognized that debates in other years might have led to an earlier glimpse of Lyndon Johnson's views on how to handle the Vietnam conflict, might have forced Richard Nixon to make public his "secret" plan for ending that conflict, and might have led to a much earlier discovery of the ramifications of the Watergate break-in. Norman Cousins has concluded that "the American people have made up their minds that the TV debates are going to be an integral part of future presidential campaigns."[28]

In the past, public pressure has played a role in candidates' decisions about whether to debate. As noted earlier, in 1960 Richard Nixon felt he had to accept Kennedy's challenge to avoid the "charge that I was afraid." In 1976, Jimmy Carter knew that, as the target of charges that he was "fuzzy" on the issues and inexperienced, he could not risk the negative impact on public opinion of a refusal to accept President Ford's debate challenge. But public opinion certainly has not always convinced the candidates to debate. In 1968, for example, with the nation torn by the Vietnam conflict, Richard Nixon and Hubert Humphrey came under growing pressure to debate. Petitions were circulated calling for debate, and newspaper editorials chastized the candidates for being unwilling to appear jointly before the public.[29] The campaign was close, however, and neither candidate seemed eager to risk a confrontation.

Public opinion might be made more effective if it were able to concentrate on a regular event. In the past, there often have been numerous debate proposals and a flood of challenges and counterchallenges, with the result that if no debate is held it often has been unclear which candidate is at fault. If a series of debates were to be formally "convened" each presidential campaign (by any of the entities discussed in Chapter V), however, with the general terms of the debates specified, public attention would be drawn more clearly to the candidates' responses, and one candidate's refusal to participate could not easily be ignored. Continued interest in candidate debate decisions by influential groups such as the League of Women Voters and support by media editorial writers would exert additional public pressure on the candidates.

Looking ahead to 1980, NBC's Edwin Newman believes that President Carter cannot refuse to debate because of the negative impact such a refusal would have on public opinion. "If he refuses," says Newman, "he will appear to be afraid, pompous, or uppity, or whatever. . . . It seems to me he's trapped."[30] If President Carter does agree to debate in 1980, it is not likely that his opponent would refuse, and two consecutive presidential elections featuring televised debates might further increase future public expectations. Two years after the first televised presidential debates, one observer wrote:

> If another round of debates attracts the kind of interest and attention that those of 1960 did, and if President Kennedy smashes the notion that an incumbent President is above debate, then it will be very difficult for any future presidential candidate to refuse to meet his opponent in face-to-face discussion. . . . [31]

This thought could be equally applicable today.

The likelihood of future televised encounters between presidential candidates might be increased in other ways as well. Television time could be set aside for debate whether or not both candidates eventually agree to debate. If only one candidate agrees, that candidate would then be given all of the time. Thus, even if adverse public opinion does not bother a candidate, the thought of an opponent having use of all that free television time may bother him enough to increase the likelihood of an acceptance. Malcom Moos, the originator of this gentle blackmail, suggested that the plan be accomplished by having Congress require the networks to allocate time for debates, and presumably, to alter or waive Section 315 at the same time.[32]

If candidates are not swayed by public opinion or by the thought of their opponents having free television time, it has been suggested that they be required by law to participate in televised debates. James Karayn, for example, has written that "every candidate for the Presidency should be obliged to present himself to the public for their inspection. . . . I think it is not too much to ask the men who are applying for the highest job in the land that they confront one another in a public forum. . . ."[33] Others might contend, to the contrary, that it is inappropriate to restrict the discretion of presidential candidates; if they cannot be trusted to conduct a campaign in the public interest, how can they be trusted with the future of the country? The more a candidate's discretion is restricted, the less likely it is that the candidate's real character and ability will be reflected in the campaign.

Even were it deemed advisable to require candidates to debate or appear on television, such a requirement would probably be found unconstitutional. The First Amendment prohibits government interference with freedom of speech, one aspect of which is the choice of whether to speak at all. The Supreme Court has held, for example, that schoolchildren cannot be compelled to join a flag salute ceremony and that motorists cannot be required to display a license plate bearing a political slogan ("Live Free or Die"), both of which were forms of required speech.[34]

A candidate's campaign is not only a form of speech but one of the most sensitive forms. As the Supreme Court has said, "it can hardly be doubted that the [First Amendment] has its fullest and most urgent application precisely to the conduct of campaigns for political office."[35] The Court has indicated that restrictions on a candidate's freedom to conduct a campaign as he sees fit, even when "neutral as to the ideas expressed" in the campaign, nevertheless go to the " 'core of our electoral process and First Amendment freedoms.' "[36]

In a 1976 decision in the case of *Buckley v. Valeo,* the Supreme Court struck down limitations on the amount of money that candidates for federal office could spend in their campaigns (although it upheld spending restrictions when candidates choose the option of receiving federal funding for their campaigns). The language it used in doing so appears to cast doubt on the permissibility of any proposal to require that candidates debate:

> In the free society ordained by our Constitution, it is not the government but the people—individually as citizens and candidates and collectively as associations and political committees—who must retain control over the quantity and range of debate on public issues in a political campaign.[37]

Thus, the public might compel candidates to debate by making clear their displeasure with those who refuse, but Congress is not likely to be able to legislate participation.

Money has been considered a means of getting candidates to debate; it has been suggested that entitlement to federal campaign funds should be conditioned on a candidate's willingness to participate in televised debate. As discussed earlier, in 1976 candidates for the presidency had the choice of either accepting federal funds for their general election campaign, in which case they had to adhere to federal spending limitations, or continuing to raise their own campaign funds. Both candidates chose the federal funding option. If Congress were persuaded that televised presidential debates were important to an informed electorate and were not likely to occur regularly otherwise, it might amend the campaign laws to make these federal funds available only to candidates who have agreed to appear in televised debates. Such a law would make a candidate think long and hard before refusing to participate, and, thus, is an attractive means of ensuring future debates without making participation a legal requirement. But imposing such severe monetary sanctions would raise the question of constitutionality almost to the same extent as a direct requirement that a candidate debate.

While it has been established that Congress is not required to fund the campaigns of all candidates, it is doubtful that it can base a distinction on whether or not a candidate chooses to exercise what is, as discussed above, a constitutionally protected right not to debate. In some cases, Congress has been able to require that individuals forgo certain protected rights in order to receive government benefits; for example, people wishing to be civil service employees must forgo participation in political campaigning.[38] But in these instances, the restrictions have had a purpose other than to compel the abandonment of a right; the restriction on civil service employees, for example, was upheld as necessary to assure an unpoliticized, efficient civil service. The restriction on access to federal funding for candidates who would not debate, however, would have as its sole purpose the coercion of the candidates to relinquish their right not to debate, and thus is likely to be struck down.

Although outright requirements and funding coercion by government probably will not pass constitutional muster, the political parties could, if they chose to do so, require or coerce their presidential candidates to participate in televised debates. The national committees of the Republican and Democratic parties could, for example, adopt rules that required their nominees to engage in televised debates as a condition of being the party's standard-bearer. If the parties did not wish to go this far, they might at least agree to require candidates for their nomination to state publicly whether they would debate if nominated. Any such measure would, of course, go well beyond any present party control over candidates and, therefore, may be unlikely as a practical matter.

Unless a better way can be found, candidate participation in televised debates will continue to depend on political judgments. However, greater efforts at public persuasion, perhaps laced with the threat of free television time for an unwilling candidate's opponent, may attract reluctant candidates to future debates.

VII/The Role of Minor Party or Independent Candidates

In 1960 and 1976, the Democratic and Republican candidates participated in televised presidential debates, but in 1960, at least sixteen—and in 1976, at least thirteen—other candidates were on various state ballots.[1] An important issue for future debates is whether and to what extent such minor party or independent candidates for president should have an opportunity to participate in televised debates.

In 1976, minor party and independent candidates objected strongly not only to their exclusion from the debates between the Republican and Democratic candidates but also to the refusal of the networks to grant them equivalent television exposure. Eugene McCarthy (an independent candidate), the Socialist Workers party, the American party, and Lester Maddox (candidate of the American Independent party) challenged this exclusion either before the FCC, the federal courts, or both.

The candidates who were excluded argued that the commission's decision in the *Aspen* case (exempting debates from the "equal time" requirement) extended only to debates that did not serve the interests of particular candidates, whereas the debates held by the League of Women Voters clearly served the interests of the Republican and Democratic candidates at the expense of the other candidates. They also claimed that, although under the *Aspen* decision neither the candidates nor the networks were to have any role in the organization of exempt debates, both Ford and Carter had been consulted about the format of the debates by the League and that the networks had played a substantial role in the affairs, as demonstrated by the 26-minute delay in the first debate. Finally, they argued that limiting the debates to major candidates violated their freedom of speech by effectively barring them from reaching the voters.

The FCC rejected all of these arguments.[2] The commission concluded that some limited candidate participation in choosing the format for
debates made them no less "bona fide news events" and that there was
no evidence of network control over the League debates. The courts
refused to overturn this determination and, without opinion, rejected
the freedom of speech claim.[3] As the law now stands, therefore, the
League of Women Voters or a similar organization may conduct debates between just the Republican and Democratic candidates, and the
television networks and other broadcasters may broadcast these debates without incurring an "equal time" obligation to minor party or
independent candidates.

In the 1978 elections, the League organized numerous debates
among candidates for lesser offices under these same principles. For
example, a League affiliate in Wisconsin organized a debate between
the Republican and Democratic candidates for governor of that state
but did not invite the Socialist Workers party candidate; the debate
was to be televised by the statewide noncommercial television network. When the excluded candidate complained to the FCC, the commission advised the candidate that

[B]roadcasting coverage of the debates could be . . . exempt from equal
opportunities requirements, pursuant to the Commission's ruling in *Aspen*
. . . [and] the Commission cannot compel the League of Women
Voters to invite a particular candidate to participate in a series of debates
nor can it require any candidate to appear to debate any other candidate.[4]

Even though the FCC and the courts do not appear likely to direct
minor party or independent candidate participation, the roles of these
candidates in any future televised presidential debates warrant further
consideration. There is little support for the proposition that *all* minor
party or independent candidates should be included in televised debates. Many of the candidates on the various state ballots are obscure
contenders representing relatively small groups of people interested in
narrow issues (for example, the Vegetarian party or the Prohibition
party candidates). Were they all to appear together, the event would be
at best a convention, certainly not a debate. Were they all given "equal
time" to use in some other way, the burden on the networks would be
intolerable, which is precisely why the "equal time" requirement was
amended in 1959, suspended in 1960, and repealed by the House or
Senate on a number of occasions (and twice by both).

The real question, therefore, is not whether *all* candidates should be
included in debates—clearly they should not—but rather whether
some—those who can by some rational test be deemed "significant" or
"substantial"—should be able to participate in debates with the major
party candidates. Further, if these candidates are included, should

they participate in all the debates or only in some. Similarly, if otherwise qualifying candidates are excluded from the debates because the major parties refuse to debate with them, should the excluded candidates be given "equal time"?

The argument against participation by even the most significant of the minor party or independent candidates centers on the concept of the two-party system under which third parties or independent candidates simply do not have sufficient significance by virtually any test to warrant inclusion in debates. Indeed, no minor party or independent candidate has ever won a presidential election or even come close. Since 1832, only nine such candidates out of literally hundreds have been able to carry even a single state.[5] In the twentieth century, minor party candidates have received electoral votes in only three out of nineteen elections, and even then, the number received was insignificant.[6] Only once did a minor party candidate receive as much as one-fourth of the popular vote, and that was Theodore Roosevelt, running as a Progressive party candidate after serving as president (1901–08) while a Republican.[7]

In 1976, Eugene McCarthy was the only minor party or independent candidate whose name appeared on the ballot in enough states to give him even a theoretical possibility of winning the election; despite considerable publicity from his efforts to block the Carter-Ford debates, McCarthy received only about 1 percent of the popular vote and no electoral votes. To have included McCarthy, Lester Maddox, or any other minor party or independent candidates in the Carter-Ford debates, the argument goes, would have given them an importance far out of proportion to their true importance. Jules Witcover and Jack Germond observed that "clearly it would have been a distortion of the political realities and an inhibition to the dialogue between Ford and Carter" to include minor party or independent candidates in the debates.[8] The same point was made by Charles Seipman shortly after the 1960 debates:

> [I]t seems sheer sentimentality to allow concern for such political minorities . . . to blind us to the fact that ours, at present, is a two-party system and that, in an election year, clarification of the conflicting policies of the major parties is the paramount consideration. If total exclusion from the air of all these minorities is necessary, the price does not seem too high. Their death knell will not thereby be rung, for the claim that publicity, these days, is the condition of party survival is to pay the hucksters too generous a compliment. The growth of a party, like its birth, stems from the incentive to common action of people's associated needs. As people sense such needs, they will organize to see them satisfied.[9]

On the other hand, to others, excluding *significant* minor party or independent candidates from such television exposure as the debates is unfair, is likely to sound the death knell of dissent, and, even if our political system is indeed a two-party system, is likely to make the Republican and Democratic parties *the* two parties. The Twentieth Century Fund Commission on Campaign Costs in 1969 said as much when it suggested ensuring at least some television time not only for major party candidates but also for minor party and independent candidates:

> In our relatively short history as a nation, ideas brought forth on the fringes of our political life have often become, in time, doctrine for the dominant center. Thus, railroad regulation, the encouragement of cooperatives and labor unions, high standards for civil service, and many other ideas first advanced by the Populists and Progressives have gained general acceptance. . . .
>
> *   *   *
>
> The Commission believes, then, that we must recognize dual needs: the preservation of a two-party system on the one hand, and an opportunity for dissent and flexibility on the other. What we do seek is the interplay of ideas—a healthy chance for the upward movement of new parties and candidates and the possible decline of the old, as well as the stability provided by a strong two-party system.[10]

The federal campaign laws make it far more difficult for minor party or independent candidates than for the major parties to obtain federal campaign funding. It has been argued that stacking the deck against them further by excluding those candidates from television time that is made available to major party candidates threatens to obliterate them entirely. Roscoe Barrow, a professor of law, has written:

> Now that the television networks can cover presidential debates between the two major party candidates, the Democratic and Republican parties, as a practical matter, are established permanently in a two-party political system. It will not be possible for any third party to develop and compete for a position as a major party.[11]

This position is supported by the fact that when Congress suspended the "equal time" law in 1960, making it lawful for the radio and television networks to provide time for the Republican and Democratic candidates, while excluding other candidates, the amount of time made available to minor party candidates dropped by more than 90 percent from the levels of the preceding election.[12] Although the *Aspen* decision does not affect other types of appearances and would not have this impact, this fact may indicate that little time will be given voluntarily to minor party or independent candidates. Critics of the exclusion policy also note the testimony of the president of one of the networks before Congress, who said that had the "equal time" provision been revoked in 1972, the network would have given eight hours of television time to the Republican and Democratic candidates, and "like an hour, maybe" to George C. Wallace, who had received more than 13 percent of the vote in 1968 and who the preelection polls had indicated would receive as much as 25 percent of the vote in 1972.[13]

The combination of the media disadvantage of minor party candidates excluded from debates or similar opportunities and the financial disadvantage they perceive under the campaign funding laws is seen by some not only as bad public policy but also as so great a handicap as to constitute an unconstitutional interference with the freedom of speech and right of assembly of members of such parties. Professor Jerome Barron has argued that the exclusion of minor party candidates from televised debates "should be viewed as presenting a fundamental challenge to the constitutional status of political freedom in America."[14] The chairman of the House Subcommittee on Communications, Congressman Lionel Van Deerlin, has agreed, stating that if minor party candidates are excluded "you shut out third-party candidates. And I think that is unconstitutional."[15] Although no court has issued an opinion dealing directly with access to televised debates, the unsuccessful challenge by McCarthy and others to their exclusion from League-sponsored debates in 1976 suggests that there is little judicial support for the proposition that exclusion is unconstitutional. As discussed above, this is likely to be the case whether or not the government is involved in presenting the debates, although the question might be somewhat more difficult if federal funds were used to pay for the debates.

If significant minor party or independent candidates are to be included in televised debates, standards must be found by which to judge the significance of a candidate. Tests of candidate significance have been devised for related areas and may provide some guidance. For example, the Twentieth Century Fund Commission on Campaign Costs, in its proposal to make free television time available to all significant candidates, established three categories of parties: (1) candidates of parties that appear on the ballot in at least three quarters of the states (provided the states represented enough electoral votes to constitute a majority in the electoral college) and that have placed first or second in the popular vote in two of the last three elections; (2) candidates of parties that meet the "three quarters of the states" test and received one-eighth of the popular vote in the last presidential election; and (3) candidates of parties that meet the "three quarters of the states" test but not the requirements of the other categories. Parties in the first category were to receive the full amount of free time (which the commission called "voters' time") while those in the other categories were to receive lesser amounts.

Professor Barrow similarly has suggested a set of categories for the purposes of determining television time: (1) major party candidates—

those parties that received 3 percent of the vote in the last election; (2) minor party candidates—those parties that received 1 percent of the vote in the last election; and (3) new party or independent candidates— supported by petitions signed by 1.5 percent of the electorate (which would qualify the candidate as a minor party candidate). According to Barrow, only six minor party candidates would have met the 3 percent test during this century,[16] and twelve candidates would have met the 1 percent test, including Eugene McCarthy in 1976.[17]

Other possible tests for distinguishing among candidates include the one used in the federal law providing funding of presidential campaigns; the law defines major parties as those whose candidates received 25 percent or more of the vote in the last presidential election, and makes minor party candidates eligible for federal campaign funds if they have obtained a place on the ballot in ten or more states.[18] The FCC's rules now provide that a presidential candidate is to be considered entitled to "equal time" nationally if the candidate has qualified for a place on the ballot in ten or more states or has made a "substantial showing" of a write-in candidacy in ten or more states.[19] Other methods for determining "significance" also have been suggested, including the use of poll results or a survey of leading journalists and political analysts.[20]

Candidates meeting the test of significance might be granted participation in all debates with major party candidates, participation in some of the debates, participation in a debate with other minor party or independent candidates, or simply time to address the public alone. Distinctions might also be made among the "significant" candidates through a hierarchical categorization similar to the plan proposed by the Commission on Campaign Costs.

The 1964 Report by the American Political Science Association's Commission on Presidential Debates suggested that there be seven presidential debates, including one devoted entirely to minority party candidates.[21] This concept of devoting one of a series of debates to minor party or independent candidates has been endorsed editorially by The New York Times.[22] Similarly, James Karayn has suggested that one or two debates be held among the "viable" minor party candidates. Herbert Gans prefers two debates with all the significant candidates, including the major party candidates, and separate debates featuring only the major party candidates. Charles Seipman has suggested simply giving significant minor party candidates excluded from debates the time they would be entitled to under the "equal time" provision to do with as they please.[23] Professor Barrow likewise would provide qualifying candidates not included in the debates with time of their own. Those meeting his "major party" test would receive "equal time" if not included in the debates, while candidates meeting the minor party test would be given one-half as much time.[24]

Unless candidate participation is somehow made compulsory, however, it would be possible to include significant minor party or independent candidates only with the agreement of the major party candidates. Since the major party candidates are likely to be better known and well ahead of the minor party or independent candidates in the polls, both major party candidates are not likely to agree. In 1976, it was clear that Jimmy Carter would not have debated had Eugene McCarthy been included. In 1968, one reason no debates were held was Hubert Humphrey's insistence that George Wallace be included in a debate and Richard Nixon's refusal to agree to this condition.[25] Thus, as a practical matter, third-party candidates deemed significant are likely to be limited to debates among themselves or to the use of some other form of television exposure.

In 1976, Eugene McCarthy wrote to the League of Women Voters asking to be included in the debates. The League responded that it was "in the process of considering a fifth debate for those presidential candidates who are on the ballot in a substantial number of states so that those individuals can have an opportunity to present their views to the public."[26] The League never held that fifth debate and never fully explained how that decision was reached; by the next series of presidential debates, however, the role of the minor party or independent candidate must be fully addressed.

VIII/Questions of Format

Each televised presidential debate has created a growing number of armchair format critics, both professional and amateur. Questions concerning the setting in which candidates should meet, how often they should meet, for how long, in whose company, and for what purpose have drawn comment from many quarters, and are the subject of substantial research and study.[1]

Much of the criticism of past formats stems from the fact that the events generally are judged by two standards, both of which may be inappropriate. Professional journalists, many of whom have followed the campaign and the candidates for months before the debates begin, judge the format by its ability to produce something "new," even though there is little that would be "new" at that point. The public tends to judge the debates by the same standards it applies to the entertainment programming normally found on television in the same time periods. But whatever standards they use, everyone seems to have suggestions for changes in debate formats; a Gallup survey after the 1976 debates indicated that about one-half of those expressing an opinion on the matter favored some changes in format.[2]

James Karayn has summarized what should be the goal in seeking a format for televised presidential debates:

> The task is to devise a format where the viewer/voter can come away with some insights and knowledge about the candidates he would not have gotten from his other "exposures" to them, be it the nightly news campaign reports, the Sunday afternoon panel show appearances, the paid political spots, or what others write about them.[3]

If the format of the debates performs this function, the debates should do much to fill what F. Clifton White has called the "basic requirement" for the electoral process—"competition of ideas, philosophies, and personalities in a manner which allows the people to make a judgment between those competitive ideas and personalities."[4]

In past televised presidential debates, the formats have resulted from negotiation and compromise among and between political candidates, broadcast networks, and, in 1976, a public service organization. Not surprisingly, the candidates have made their format decisions—just as they have made their initial decisions as to whether to debate—on the basis of what appears most to their advantage. In 1960, for example, Richard Nixon preferred to have only a few televised debates because he believed that he could deliver a "knockout" blow to the inexperienced John Kennedy and did not want to give Kennedy a chance to recover in a long series of debates. Kennedy, on the other hand, wanted at least five debates because he believed that he would gain slowly whenever he and Nixon were seen together.

Even when formats are agreed upon, candidates are cautious about their participation. "There are no winners," observes Professor Nelson Polsby, "just losers, those who say something . . . that sends the press baying like a pack of beagles into the next week . . . seeking after 'clarifications,' revisions, apologies, or concessions."[5] Winning the debates may be important to the candidates, but not losing is even more important.

Given these pressures on format and conduct, it is no wonder that prior debates have been criticized by many observers for not fully ventilating campaign issues. Nonetheless, without a requirement that candidates debate, or an exceptionally strong incentive for them to do so, candidates are likely to continue to make designation of an acceptable format a condition of their participation. This means that as a practical matter the choice of formats will be limited to those that do not subject the candidates to unacceptable risks by forcing them to discuss issues they do not wish to discuss or appear in situations they believe likely to emphasize their weakest rather than their strongest characteristics. It also means that no single format can be chosen for all future debates since what is acceptable to candidates one year may be unacceptable to those who are candidates four years later. Within these constraints of practicality, however, there remain numerous choices.

To Debate or Not To Debate

Should the debates, in fact, be debates? The traditional debate format is a regulated confrontation between matched contestants who are given equal and adequate time to present their positions on a stated proposition to an audience who will then be able to make a decision on the presentation and merits of the positions.[6]

In collegiate team debating, where many candidates have been intro-
duced to debates, the format generally is as follows:

Two teams of speakers are always involved: an affirmative team defends a
controversial proposition, and a negative team opposes it. Each team is giv-
en the same amount of speaking time. Both constructive speeches and rebuttals are included. Because the affirmative has the burden of proof, it has
the privilege of presenting first and last speech. No speaker is subject to interruption, and no provision is made for the direct questioning of speakers
by opponents.[7]

The Lincoln-Douglas debates came close to the traditional debate format: The first speaker was given one hour to present his position; his
opponent then had an hour and a half to present his opinion; and the
first speaker then had one-half hour for rebuttal; there were no intervening panelists or moderators. However, while the subject of slavery
emerged as the central issue in the debates of 1858, the candidates did
not debate a proposition stated in advance. The 1960 and 1976 televised
debates were not consistent with the traditional format; they lacked direct confrontation between the candidates on issues and did not deal
with a stated proposition.

The television networks planned to model the first televised presidential debates in 1960 on the debates between Thomas Dewey and
Harold Stassen in the 1948 Oregon presidential primary. In those encounters, the first candidate was given twenty minutes for a statement;
then his opponent made a twenty-minute opening statement; this was
followed by the first candidate's eight and one-half minute rebuttal,
then the opponent's eight and one-half minute rebuttal. The candidates
discussed a single specified issue, in this case the question of outlawing
communism.

The candidates rejected this format in 1960 for a number of reasons.
First, they did not believe that it would attract and hold a television audience. The Dewey-Stassen debates themselves had been widely criticized as dull, and a similar debate between John Kennedy and Hubert
Humphrey in the West Virginia primary earlier that year also had been
deemed boring. Second, the 1960 campaign offered no clear-cut issue
that could serve as the stated proposition for a debate. Finally, the candidates' advisors cautioned that the format could lead a candidate, in
the heat of combat, to make an ill-considered remark that could have
international repercussions for the country.[8]

Instead, the networks and candidates Kennedy and Nixon negotiated a format that involved placing a moderator and panelists between
the candidates. In the first and fourth debates, each candidate was to
make an opening statement of eight minutes, followed by questions
posed to the candidates in turn by a panel of broadcast journalists, followed by a three-minute closing statement by each candidate. During

the questioning portion of the debate, each candidate would have an opportunity to comment on the answer of the other candidate. The second and third debates were similar, except the opening and closing statements were omitted. In answering questions and commenting on their opponent's answer, the candidates were limited to two and one-half minutes for the answer and one and one-half minutes for the comment.

In accepting the networks' offer of time for a debate, Richard Nixon had stated that "it should be a debate, as opposed to two people reading notes. It should be a free contest—an opportunity for each to examine the other's mind."[9] But by the time a final agreement on format had been reached, all parties recognized that the events were not debates in the traditional sense. Although NBC originally had labeled the proposed proceedings "The Great Debates," most formal network publicity in 1960 used the term "joint appearances" instead. The title card on the television screen read "Face-to-Face," and the term "joint appearance" or "discussion" was used in on-the-air references. Moderator Howard K. Smith's opening words were:

> Good evening. The television and radio stations of the United States . . . are proud to provide facilities for a discussion of issues in the current political campaign by the two major candidates for the presidency. . . . In this, the first discussion in a series of four joint appearances, the subject matter has been agreed. . . .

The 1976 debates followed much the same format. Each candidate was given three minutes to answer a question posed by a panel of journalists and two and one-half minutes to respond to any follow-up question from the panel; the other candidate was then given two minutes to comment on this answer. Each candidate was given three minutes at the end of the session to deliver a summation.

There was growing interest in 1976 in at least some type of direct conversation between the candidates. Before the debates even began, Jimmy Carter stated his view that the format should permit the candidates to question each other as well as to submit to questioning by others.[10] After the first debate, which was widely termed "dull" by critics, Carter reiterated his preference for direct questioning, but the format remained the same.

In an effort to introduce some element of a direct confrontation into the proceedings, the panelists chosen for the final debate agreed among themselves in advance that when they were given the signal by the moderator to ask final questions, they would request instead that each candidate put a question to the other. Thus, panelist Joseph Kraft proposed to ask Carter, "After months of campaigning against President

Ford, isn't there something you'd like to say to him now?'' Through an oversight, however, the panelists were not given the warning that the program was drawing to a close, and time ran out before they could implement their plan. The three presidential debates of 1976 were dubbed "a joint press conference" by one of the panelists.[11]

Proponents of the use of a format including at least some form of direct confrontation between the candidates contend that it would tend to sharpen the issues in a campaign. One study points out, for example, that debates can be an unusually efficient way for a voter to compile information about electoral alternatives. Without debates, a voter must cull information from numerous, often one-sided presentations, such as newspaper and television advertisements and news reports of candidate speeches, a task that requires considerable effort. "It is no wonder," concludes the study, "that many people short-circuit this arduous data collection and processing task by allowing their prior partisan identifications (and thus their selective biases) to guide their choice of behavior."[12] While the 1960 and 1976 debates indicated that the joint presentation of the candidates could make the voter's job easier, the study concluded that the debates would be even more effective with direct confrontation:

> [T]he candidates might be allowed to engage in fuller immediate exchange of views rather than simply side-by-side pronouncements on the same issue in formal, consecutive fashion. What the debate formats lack thus far is a way to sharpen the differences through more immediate give-and-take. Such an exchange need not approach the pinnacle of socratic dialogue to serve this information-cost-reducing function of voters more fully. But with an increasingly well-educated and issue-oriented electorate, this is a direction in which future debate planning might move.[13]

A format in which the candidates challenge each other also appears to be the choice of voters. Public opinion surveys made shortly after the 1976 debates indicated that most persons with an opinion on the format of the debates would prefer a direct exchange between the candidates.[14] Editorializing in favor of this type of format, the *Washington Star* noted that the "press conference format" of 1960 and 1976 tended to encourage "stodginess" and discourage viewers.[15] An exchange between the candidates, it is argued, would draw and keep viewers, thereby enhancing what may be one of the most important functions of the debates—forcing on the viewer at least a glimpse of the character and views of the opponent of the candidate he believes he favors. NBC correspondent Edwin Newman, a participant in the 1976 debates, observed that "the great advantage of the so-called debate format . . . is that it appears to be dramatic and it leads people to watch. . . ."[16]

For every proponent of direct exchange between candidates in any future televised presidential debates, there is someone who would argue that less emphasis on confrontation would be an improvement. A real debate, it is said, requires a narrow, clear-cut issue on which contrasting views are likely to be expressed; without such an issue, the "debate" becomes too dull to hold television viewers. Moreover, even where clear-cut issues do exist, political candidates generally believe that the public is not won over by a candidate who attacks his opponent, a belief borne out by polls and experience. The candidates' surveys in 1976 indicated that Jimmy Carter harmed himself each time he appeared to attack Gerald Ford in the debates and that attacks on the Democrats by vice-presidential candidate Robert Dole in the vice-presidential debate did the Republicans more harm than good. A debate that emphasizes confrontation but is held between candidates who are reluctant to compete strongly with each other is likely to be dull and insipid.

Others opposed to a debate format featuring added confrontation are concerned that candidates will end up in a "shooting match" in which a trailing candidate may be tempted to seek to embarrass the other candidate in order to reverse the election trend. Confrontation also is said to encourage the win-lose syndrome that already permeates the events, a result that is contrary to the real goal of ventilating issues and exposing character. Harvey Wheeler pointed out after the 1960 debates that a televised fight between candidates is of little value:

> What we are after is not a spectacle of candidates for our highest office wrangling with each other. What we require is a mode of electoral competition through which the opposing candidates are induced to develop competing overall programs for dealing with the problems of our nation. . . . It is not really necessary to this process that the competing candidates ever actually interrogate each other personally or directly. What must be emphasized is not the competition between personalities, but the competition between programs and policies.[17]

Moreover, the debate format has little, if any, relevance to the qualifications for the office of president. "[T]he capacity to debate is of negligible relevance in actually governing," writes Professor Polsby.[18] Talents such as dealing with the bureaucracy, choosing presidential advisors, negotiating with opponents, and the ability to work hard and effectively are not tested by the debate format. Polsby points out that while in the parliamentary system "bashing the opposition in oral debate" is viewed as a skill, the American system of government, one in which the challenge often is to blur the differences of opinion between factions in an effort to find a common ground, finds such skills of little use. Similarly, Daniel Boorstin concluded:

[O]f course, a man's ability, while standing under klieg lights without notes, to answer in two and a half minutes a question kept secret until that moment, had only the most dubious relevance—if any at all—to his real qualifications to make deliberate presidential decisions on long-standing public questions after being instructed by a corps of advisors.[19]

Aversion to a debate format, even in its 1960 and 1976 form, has generated suggestions for other formats that deviate even further from the traditional debate. For example, Professor Polsby urges adoption of what amounts to a conversation format, which he justifies this way:

The spontaneous capabilities of a candidate's mind can be discovered far more successfully in conversation, where entitlement to the floor is subject to tacit negotiation, moment by moment, where interruptions are possible, and where all parties to the interaction are responsible for its content, and the straightjacket of question-and-answer gives way to a more freely flowing sort of discussion. Skill at this sort of conversation is, moreover, far more relevant to the conduct of the presidency, because these are the sorts of interactions a President must have in order to do his job.[20]

It is interesting to note that in his 1960 magazine article calling for presidential debates Adlai Stevenson also suggested a format that was more conversation than debate oriented. "I don't mean 'debate' in the literal collegiate sense of the word," Stevenson said, "but a sustained discussion."[21]

A similar suggestion has been made by Max Frankel of *The New York Times*, a panelist in the second 1976 debate. Frankel envisions a roundtable discussion among two candidates and two questioners. This format would resemble the 1968 debate between Robert Kennedy and Eugene McCarthy in the California presidential primary, where the candidates sat at a table with three ABC correspondents who asked them questions, with time given to each candidate to comment on the answers of the other.

Another suggested format, even farther afield from the traditional debate, is presenting the candidates in separate back-to-back programs. This would eliminate all aspects of a confrontation but, in theory, would allow television viewers to compare the candidates by seeing one after the other. Similar proposals would have the candidates appear in succeeding interview programs such as "Meet the Press" or "Issues and Answers."

The various opinions about the appropriate format for televised presidential encounters run the spectrum from traditional head-to-head debates to separate but equal back-to-back programs, suggesting that there may be no "right" format. Instead, it may be that future presidential debates should consist of a number of different debates with different formats or that the format in each case should be tailored to the circumstances of the election year.

Panelists and Moderators

Deciding on the appropriate role and composition of a panel of questioners is part of the problem of choosing a format. If future debates are to be direct encounters between candidates, there would, of course, be no need for such a panel. If questions are to be put to the candidates by others, the panel aspect of the debates must be considered.

The idea of having persons other than the candidates and perhaps a moderator appear in the debate programs originated with the broadcast networks in 1960. Each debate that year involved a moderator and a panel of broadcast and print journalists. The first and last debates used panels composed of network correspondents, with ABC, CBS, NBC, and the Mutual Radio Network each choosing a panelist. At the insistence of the candidates, the panels for the second and third debates included representatives of the print media chosen by the candidates' press secretaries by lot from among the reporters traveling with the candidates.

In 1976, the panelists included one broadcast journalist, one newspaper or wire service journalist, and one individual from the editorial side of journalism. The League chose the panelists from lists of fifty persons in each of these three categories compiled by each candidate or from lists that it had compiled itself.[22] In both 1960 and 1976, the candidates welcomed the addition of the panelists, whose presence prevented either of the candidates from appearing overly aggressive; as mentioned above, candidates have long believed that a candidate who appears aggressive or who attacks another candidate is risking injury in the public estimation.

The presence of a panel provides some assurance that the candidates do not avoid what might be termed "no win" issues—those issues that cannot be addressed without alienating some substantial portion of the electorate (for example, the question of abortion). Although neither candidate would wish to direct the debates into such an area, a panelist might do so. The presence of a panel also may provide some useful control over the proceedings. Robert Sarnoff of NBC stated in 1960 that the use of a panel was "a disciplined, clear-cut method of pitting the candidates' arguments against each other—which is after all the quintessence of debates—while minimizing the formalities and flourishes that debaters are prone to indulge in at the expense of the issues themselves."[23]

On the other hand, the presence of panelists has been attacked on a number of grounds. In 1960, for example, one critic referred to the news reporters who were participating as "a clutter of egomaniacs of the news media."[24] Panelists also can become commentators: Joseph Kraft, a panelist in the final 1976 debate, referred to President Ford's record as "rotten" and observed that Ford was "obsessed with saving money."[25] Panelists have also been criticized for drawing the candidates into areas where some feel they should not tread. Both James Reston and Arthur Krock of *The New York Times* have suggested that during the 1960 debates panelists lead the discussion into "strategic plans for dealing with Cuba and Quemoy and Matsu," subjects that had "no proper place in a political campaign."[26]

The selection of newspaper or broadcast journalists as panelists has also been subject to criticism. Reporters, it is said, are too "news" oriented, especially those who travel with the presidential campaigns. They become caught up in the reporting of the campaign, and seem often to overlook issues of concern to the public. Thus, some observers would prefer to replace journalist panelists with "expert" panelists; for example, persons selected for their familiarity with economic issues or urban problems. The problem with experts, however, is that they, like some journalists, may well be tempted to use the occasion to expound their own views, theories, or biases; moreover, they may not be adept at framing questions and could be flustered before the television cameras.

Others would replace, or at least augment, journalists with members of Congress; the congressional leadership, for example, might be invited to pose questions. In fact, Theodore White has suggested that a presidential debate be held as part of a joint session of Congress, with an opportunity for participation by the Congress. Another possibility is that the candidates could appear in debates with advisors—perhaps those they would consider nominating to Cabinet positions if elected; the advisors could direct questions to the other candidate or respond to questions along with their candidate.

Other suggestions also have merit—and present problems. Representatives of special interest segments of the public (the AFL-CIO or NAACP, for example) might be given the opportunity to pose questions of particular interest to their groups. Even more than in the case of experts, however, these persons could be expected to use the exposure as an opportunity to argue their own point of view. In 1960, the networks and candidates came under considerable pressure from many interest groups, particularly civil rights groups, to include them in the panels, but these requests were rejected for fear that the debates would be used as a soapbox by special interest panelists.[27] Members of the public, chosen by lot or chance without regard to purported expertise or institutional affiliation, also might be given an opportunity to participate.

The choice of a moderator for the debates has raised similar questions. In 1960, each of the four debate moderators was chosen by the network charged with the responsibility for producing the debate on behalf of all the networks. The networks originally proposed to choose a moderator who was an outstanding jurist, college president, or other prominent person, but the candidates demanded a broadcast professional who, they felt, would be much less likely to impose his or her own beliefs and personality on the debates.[28] After studying the 1960 debates, the American Political Science Association Commission on Presidential Debates suggested that the networks' original suggestion would have been preferable and that moderators should be drawn from the ranks of the Supreme Court, educators, members of Congress, Nobel prize winners, or former presidents. The candidates' position on the subject does have merit, however, for a renowned moderator is indeed more likely to take attention from the candidates and may not have the skills necessary to keep the debates within their time limits and the debaters on the designated issues.

Choosing the Subject

The subject matter for future debates is another issue that must be carefully examined. In both 1960 and 1976, negotiations between the candidates and the debate organizers resulted in the designation of one debate to deal with domestic policy issues and another to deal with foreign policy issues; in the remaining debates, the panelists could ask questions in any area they wished. The great range of subjects covered was a result of the broad designations "domestic" and "foreign policy" and the absence of any subject designation for the other debates. In the 1976 debates, for example, as many as fifty questions were posed during the course of the four and one-half hours, and the League concluded that "the choice of subjects was such that almost every important current issue [was] dealt with at some point."

Dealing with "almost every important current issue" is, however, not very useful if they are dealt with superficially. In order to ensure more depth in the treatment of important issues, James Karayn has suggested that each debate be confined to a broad subject area and that discussion during the debate be limited to a very few topics chosen from within that area. Karayn suggests debates devoted to foreign and domestic policy and to the candidates' perceptions of the role of the office of president. In 1960, the networks also sought to interest the candidates in discussing specific propositions; the candidates, however, insisted that topic designations could be no narrower than "domestic" or "foreign." Frank Stanton of CBS disagreed with the candidates' decision:

Since the political history of this country has always focused on a few fundamental issues, I believe that it would be most desirable to have some debates on single issues. Such discussions, in depth and at length, could be the single most powerful force in educating our citizens during the campaign and the effect would hold over long after the election.[29]

A survey of numerous studies of the 1960 debates concluded that the debates would have been more effective in presenting the issues to the voters had each debate been limited to a single topic.[30]

The question of who should participate in picking debate subjects is part of the same format issue. In both 1960 and 1976, the panelists chose the specific issues within the broad topic designations of the candidates. The American Political Science Association Commission concluded that the candidates should have a substantial role in the selection of debate issues since the election campaign is, to an extent, defined by those choices. The commission also suggested, however, that within the topical areas chosen by the candidates it might be appropriate for a committee of experts to select specific issues.[31] Walter Mears has suggested that a group of journalists, economists, foreign policy experts, and, perhaps, representatives of the voting public devise the agenda for the debates.[32]

The suggestion that the public have a role in choosing debate issues may first have been made by Richard Nixon in 1960. During the discussion of whether or not there would be a fifth debate that year, Nixon instead suggested lengthening the fourth debate by one hour to allow the public to question the candidates. To facilitate this, Nixon proposed to set up microphones and cameras in specified locations throughout the country.[33]

Others have suggested that the public be polled to determine the issues of the greatest importance to them and that those issues be made the subject of any future debates. For example, in 1976 Daniel Yankelovich, Cyrus Vance, and others formed an organization, The Public Agenda, to survey national leaders and citizens to determine which current issues are of greatest public concern. The Public Agenda organization conducted such a survey prior to the election and conferred with Ford and Carter aides concerning the results in an effort to ensure that the election campaign would address the public's concerns. Use of public polling in choosing debate topics offers the advantage of involving the public in the proceedings to a greater extent—and of focusing the debate on the issues on which votes will be cast, rather than the issues of interest to political scientists.

All the panelists chosen to participate in the 1976 debates reported receiving literally hundreds of letters, telegrams, and telephone calls from persons or groups who had questions they wished the panelists to ask, indicating great public interest in the choice of debate subjects.

Number, Length, and Setting

The scheduling and number of televised presidential debates, the length of each debate, and the appropriate setting also need consideration.

There were four debates in 1960 and four in 1976, one of which was devoted to the vice-presidential candidates. These numbers have not generated controversy but may represent the maximum number of debates that can be held without greatly increasing the risk that present campaign practices will be completely replaced by televised debates. More than three or four debates would be likely to diminish public attention to other aspects of the campaign and, correspondingly, reduce the extent to which the candidates seek to present themselves to the voters in other ways. Campaign financing restrictions already have lessened the amount of "local" campaigning, reducing the neighborhood campaign offices and town square rallies that serve the purpose of keeping the candidate in some direct touch with the public.

Fewer debates, on the other hand, unless significantly lengthened, would not allow the public a sufficient opportunity to analyze the candidates and their positions carefully. Reducing the number of debates would encourage the win/lose approach to the debates and allow a minor "slip" by one of the candidates, or one fortuitous response to a question, to distort the entire election.

There are also choices to be made in the scheduling of presidential debates. It has been suggested, for example, that at least one debate should be held at the very end of the campaign, perhaps in the day or two prior to the election. If the final debate were scheduled earlier, it is argued, the candidates could then dash about the country delivering messages to special interest groups contrary to positions they took during the debates, or they could resort to mass merchandising through televised spots to influence the election on other than the substantive grounds covered by the debates. The final week of the campaign, it is said, is "the traditional period in which the real heat is put on."[34]

On the other hand, a debate at the very end of the campaign might allow candidates to make last minute changes that could not be widely challenged on the eve of the election. Moreover, as each successive day of a campaign period passes, more and more people have made up their minds about how they are going to vote. In addition, the later in a campaign a debate takes place, the more likely it is that the registration deadline in various states will have passed, thereby reducing the impact of the debates on voter turnout. In this regard, it is interesting to note that, although the 1976 debates did not appear to have a particular impact on voter turnout nationally, the voter turnout in the state of Wisconsin, where state law allows voters to register on election day, was in excess of 65 percent—11 percent higher than the national figure.[35]

There are good reasons, therefore, to have the debates both early and late in the election campaign. Perhaps the best plan, as James Karayn has suggested, is to spread debates evenly between Labor Day and Election Day.[36]

The length of each televised presidential debate is limited by two factors. The first is the finite nature of television time and the economic cost of using it. As discussed earlier, the 1960 and 1976 debates cost the television broadcast networks millions of dollars in lost revenues. While the networks do gain prestige and large audiences, and while they do have an obligation as trustees of the public's airwaves to make time available for such purposes, fairness and practicality demand that there be a limit on the amount of television time co-opted for presidential debates.

Even if the networks were to be paid for broadcast time, there is a second factor limiting televised debates—audience interest. Although, as indicated earlier, the 1960 and 1976 televised debates did not lead to significant viewer tune-out, how closely the 60- and 90-minute lengths of those debates pushed the outer limits of viewer interest is not known. Viewers are likely to have been conditioned by regular television programming to lengths rarely in excess of one hour except for action sports or a glittering TV special.

While the debates may have reached a maximum length in terms of the two factors just examined, they have provided frustratingly short opportunity for the discussion of national issues. "Reading the 1960 debates makes clear how little can be said about any important issue of domestic or foreign policy either in a short opening statement, an even shorter answer to a question, or in still shorter comments on answers."[37] The candidates' remarks in the 1960 debates were printed in normal type size in forty-six pages of a book. During the four and one-half hours of the 1976 debates, neither candidate spoke for much more than five minutes at any one time. With due regard for the practical limitations of cost and attention span, therefore, it would be constructive to give further thought to the possible lengthening of the debates or, by format changes, increasing the opportunity for the candidates to do the talking.

The final format issue is the appropriate setting for the events. The 1960 debates took place in network television studios, where advanced technology was used to ensure a quality television program and where no studio audience was in attendance. In 1976, with the networks excluded from a meaningful role in the arrangements by the *Aspen* interpretation of the "equal time" provision, the debates were held in four theaters and halls at geographically diverse locations. In addition, also as a result of the FCC ruling, a live audience was invited in order to demonstrate that the events were in fact "news events," not television programs.

While the presence of a live audience does tend to humanize a debate and make it appear less a slickly packaged television production (some persons believe that the famous "gap" in the first debate in 1976 said more about the candidates than did all the time they spent speaking), it also creates the danger, as the League recognized, that the millions of home viewers will be unfairly influenced by the small audience. The League carefully instructed the audience "to sit on their hands and keep their mouths shut" to avoid any possible influence on the viewers.[38] As one of Jimmy Carter's advisors fretted, "one frown could color the whole public reaction."[39] Since it is clear that future debates will continue to have their major impact on the home television audience, the argument that they should be held in television studios where they are more likely to be free of the complications and dangers of the live audience is persuasive. Freedom to hold the debates without a live audience and still avoid the "equal time" requirement may, however, require a further FCC ruling.

Debates and Other Programming

The place of the debates in the overall presentation of presidential candidates on television is a fundamental question that bears on the narrower questions of format. Whether the debates are the candidates only television exposure other than their own paid political advertisements or whether they are to be complemented by other types of television programming must be a factor in deciding on format.

In 1960, for example, the networks had hoped to combine the debates with at least four hours of television programming featuring the candidates in other formats, such as appearances on "Face the Nation" or "Meet the Press." NBC originally proposed four one-hour debates and four one-hour discussion programs featuring questioning of the candidates by news reporters. CBS had proposed a total of eight hours of programming, which would have included two programs (an initial program and an election eve program) in which both candidates could make statements directly to the viewers, and six other programs that were to be a combination of debates, press interviews, and network-produced portraits of the candidates.[40]

There have been a number of suggestions for placing presidential debates within a broader context of television election programming. The commission established by the American Political Science Association, for example, recommended seven television programs between Labor Day and Election Day. The first, to be moderated by "outstanding public figures," would provide an opportunity for the presidential and vice-presidential candidates to present an "overview" of the issues as they saw them. The next four programs were envisioned as an in-depth exploration of key campaign issues with a panel of interviewers and members of Congress directing questions to the candidates. In the sixth program, the candidates of the minor parties (those on the ballot in at least ten states) would be questioned by a panel. In the final program, the presidential and vice-presidential candidates would sum up their positions on various issues. All in all, the commission "proposed a set of programs differing substantially from 1960 but, in a sense, agreeing with the viewer comments . . . more time, more specific issues, and elimination of interviewer panels" in some of the programs.[41]

James Karayn has suggested that debates between presidential candidates be preceded by separate half-hour back-to-back appearances by the candidates. These programs would substitute for the opening statements by the candidates and could provide a source of topics for questions during the debates. Karayn also suggests that there be individual interview programs with each candidate midway in the series of debate programs. This, he believes, would allow the candidates an opportunity to correct any misstatements made during the debate programs themselves and would allow the interviewers to follow up on themes only touched on in the debates. As another part of the package, Karayn proposes a program featuring a discussion between the candidates' advisors; this would allow the public to scrutinize the people who help the candidates determine their future policy positions.[42]

Other suggestions for a television "package" include Herbert Gans's proposal for two "1976 style" debates featuring all candidates who are on the ballot in one-half or more of the states; two debates with the major party candidates only; two programs with the major party candidates in a press conference type format; and a final election eve special in which all of the candidates would make final presentations.[43] Shortly after the 1960 debates, Harvey Wheeler suggested a series of four programs: the first program would allow each candidate to state his position on campaign issues; the second and third programs would feature interrogation of each candidate by a panel of journalists, economists, and political scientists; and the final program would feature a summary delivered by each candidate.[44]

After reviewing the criticism of the format of the presidential debates in 1960 and 1976, CBS's Richard Salant has concluded that "no single format can do all the things that are demanded of it" and that the solution is a mix of election programs, "each of which can supplement the others, each of which can compensate for the shortcomings of the others." Salant suggests programs in which the candidates can present their case directly to the public, joint press conferences, debates where the candidates question each other, in-depth interviews, a documentary about the candidates' origins and record, and a final program in which the candidates summarize their campaign. Salant predicts:

With that kind of mix we would not engage in endless discussion about the details of events like those sponsored by the League, because together, such a variety of broadcasts would make the whole greater than the sum of the parts. The League events would be only one of the games in town—and not the only one.[45]

Debates patterned after those of 1960 or 1976, while important sources of information that should be available through television during an election campaign, need not—indeed, should not—be the only source of that information. John Leonard of *The New York Times* has written that "what the camera can do, suggesting character, it did quite well" in the 1976 debates. "Television was telling us we can rely on Mr. Carter's (perhaps excessive) imagination and on Mr. Ford's lack of one, and that neither one was Charles de Gaulle or Winston Churchill or Leon Trotsky or Captain Kangaroo. What more can we ask . . . ?"[46] While this understates the impact and the contribution of televised presidential debates, it does remind us not to expect the debates to do everything. The continuation of televised presidential debates in future campaigns, therefore, should not mark the end of efforts to harness the power of television to serve the electoral process.

Chapter I

1. Quoted in Robert E. Sanders, "The Great Debates," Freedom of Information Center Publication No. 67 (Columbia: University of Missouri, School of Journalism, 1961), p. 1.

2. A concise history of early campaign practices and the evolution of primary elections appears in Jules Witcover, *Marathon: The Pursuit of the Presidency 1972–1976* (New York: Viking Press, 1977), pp. 20–28.

3. Theodore H. White, *The Making of the President, 1960* (New York: Atheneum Publishers, 1961), p. 279.

4. The most thorough research into the theory and practice of candidate debates in American political campaigns has been conducted by Dr. Myles Martel of West Chester State College, West Chester, Pennsylvania 19380. Dr. Martel has interviewed more than 70 persons closely involved in major candidate debates since World War II, including nine presidential candidates; he also has conducted an intensive study of the role of debates in the congressional elections of 1978. Dr. Martel defines a "political campaign debate" as "an event featuring two jointly appearing opposing candidates [where] explicit and equitable provisions are made in the format for them to refute one another without interruptions. . . ." Myles Martel, "Debates in American Political Campaigns: History, Strategy and Significance" (unpublished manuscript), p. 2.

5. Quoted in Jack Germond and Jules Witcover, "Presidential Debates: An Overview" (Paper prepared for the American Enterprise Institute Conference on the Future of Presidential Debates, Washington, D.C., October 1977), p. 4.

6. *The New York Times, The Mass Media and Politics* (New York: Arno Press, 1972), p. 37.

7. This statement was made in a 1962 NBC interview; quoted in Earl Mazo et al., "The Great Debates" (Paper prepared for the Center for the Study of Democratic Institutions, Santa Barbara: Fund for the Republic, 1962), p. 13n.

8. *Saturday Review*, November 13, 1976, p. 4.

9. Frank Stanton, "A CBS View," in *The Great Debates*, ed. Sidney Kraus (Bloomington: Indiana University Press, 1962), p. 67.

10. Elihu Katz and Jacob J. Feldman, "The Debates in the Light of Research: A Sur-

vey of Surveys," in *The Great Debates*, p. 193; *The Washington Post*, November 28, 1976, p. A7.

11. *The Washington Post*, October 1976, p. F1.

Chapter II

1. *Newsweek*, September 27, 1976, p. 33.

2. *The Mass Media and Politics*, p. 393.

3. Ibid., p. 394.

4. Ibid., p. 393.

5. Sanders, "The Great Debates," p. 1.

6. Bernard Rubin, *Political Television* (Belmont, California: Wadsworth Publishing Co., 1967), p. 21; Richard S. Salant, "The Television Debates: A Revolution That Deserves a Future," *Public Opinion Quarterly* 26 (Fall 1962), p. 346.

7. Erik Barnouw, *Tube of Plenty* (New York: Oxford University Press, 1975), p. 17.

8. H. Rep. 464, 69th Cong., 1st Sess. (1926), p. 16.

9. Samuel L. Becker and Elmer W. Lower, "Broadcasting in Presidential Campaigns," in *The Great Debates*, p. 29.

10. 47 U.S.C. §315(a).

11. *Lar Daly*, 26 F.C.C. 715 (1959).

12. When it added the exemptions from the "equal time" requirement, Congress also specified that the exemptions were "not to be construed as relieving broadcasters, in connection with the presentation of newscasts, news interviews, news documentaries, and on-the-spot coverage of news events, from the obligation imposed upon them . . . to afford reasonable opportunity for the discussion of conflicting views on issues of public importance." Pub. L. 86–274, §1, 73 Stat. 557. The obligation to broadcast conflicting views on controversial issues of public importance is known as the "fairness doctrine." The appearance of a candidate for the presidency on a television broadcast can give rise to "fairness doctrine" obligations for the broadcaster even if not covered by the "equal time" provision. The FCC has explained the applicability of "fairness" to candidates:

The fairness doctrine provides that if a broadcaster presents a discussion of one side of a controversial issue of public importance it must afford a reasonable opportunity for the presentation of contrasting points of view in its overall programming. There is no obligation under the fairness doctrine that equal time be afforded each side as would be the case where a candidate appears on a program subject to the equal opportunities requirement of Section 315. . . . Rather, the broadcaster has the discretion to determine how best to present the contrasting viewpoints on the issue; thus, it may make determinations as to the significance of contrasting viewpoints and decide which forum and format would be the most appropriate for the presentation of these views. . . .

In an election for public office each candidate cannot be considered a separate controversial issue of public importance merely by reason of his or her candidacy or partisan campaign. Rather the issue presented to the voters is who, among all the candidates, should be elected; the individual candidates represent contrasting viewpoints on that issue. Hence, under the fairness doctrine a broadcaster is required only to make a reasonable good faith judgment as to the significance of a particular candidate and decide how much broadcast coverage should be devoted to his candidacy and campaign activities. *American Independent Party*, 62 F.C.C. 2d 4, 11–12 (1976).

13. Sen. Rep. No. 562, 86th Cong., 1st Sess. (1959).

14. Becker and Lower, "Broadcasting in Presidential Campaigns," pp. 34–35.

15. From the research of Dr. Myles Martel (see note 4, Chapter I); *The New York Times*, August 18, 1940, p. 33.

16. Becker and Lower, p. 40.

17. Ibid.

18. White, *The Making of the President 1960*, p. 279.

19. Sanders, "The Great Debates," p. 4; Evron M. Kirkpatrick, "Presidential Candidate Debates: What Can We Learn From 1960?" (Paper prepared for the American Enterprise Institute Conference on the Future of Presidential Debates, Washington, D.C., October 1977), p. 3; Becker and Lower, p. 40.

20. Sanders, "The Great Debates," p. 4.

21. Rubin, *Political Television*, p. 20.

22. Pub. L. 86–77, August 14, 1960, 74 Stat, 554; 1959 U.S. Code Cong. and Adm. News, p. 2564.

23. Rubin, *Political Television*, p. 49.

24. Ibid.

25. Ibid., p. 50.

26. Kirkpatrick, "Presidential Candidate Debates: What Can We Learn From 1960?" p. 1.

27. Ibid.; Sanders, "The Great Debates," p. 1.

28. White, *The Making of the President 1960*, p. 289.

29. Ibid., p. 288.

30. Ibid., p. 294.

31. Kirkpatrick, "Presidential Candidate Debates: What Can We Learn From 1960?" p. 2n. Information about debates in other countries appears in Sig Mickelson, *The Electric Mirror* (New York: Dodd, Mead & Co., 1972), pp. 208–210. Information about post-1960 local political debates appears in "The Little Debates," *The Reporter* (December 6, 1962), pp. 36–38; in addition, the Ford Foundation and the John and Mary Markle Foundation sponsored a study of candidate debates in the 1976 and 1978 congressional and gubernatorial elections, "Campaign Debates '78: Report of the Campaign '78 Debate Survey Project," November 30, 1977 (unpublished), which concluded that debates among candidates at all levels had become increasingly popular and often were carried on radio and television. The League of Women Voters, through its state affiliates, sponsored debates among congressional and gubernatorial candidates in more than ten states in 1978, including New York, Illinois, and California.

32. A brief history of attempts to repeal or modify Section 315 appears in Nicholas Zapple, "Historical Evolvement of Section 315" (Paper prepared for the American Enterprise Institute Conference on the Future of Presidential Debates, Washington, D.C., October 1977).

33. *The Mass Media and Politics*, p. 464.

34. The FCC decision on the complaints of Congresswoman Chisholm and Mayor Yorty appears in *Section 315 Ruling*, 35 F.C.C.2d 572 (1972). Congresswoman Chisholm appealed to the United States Court of Appeals for the District of Columbia Circuit, which issued a preliminary order sustaining her position until the matter could be fully litigated (*Chisholm v. FCC*, No. 72–1505 (D.C. Cir., June 2, 1972), 24 P & F Radio Reg. 2d 206):

The question before us is essentially one of fact, namely, whether the programs in question are or are not debates, as distinct from news interviews within the meaning of the statutory exemptions. In our view, petitioner has a reasonably good chance of demonstrating on the merits that the programs in question were more akin to debates than to news interviews.

Mayor Yorty did not appeal the FCC's ruling, but apparently expected to receive the same treatment as Congresswoman Chisholm following the court's preliminary order. The FCC, however, took the position that, since it still did not believe the "equal time" requirement was applicable, it would interpret the court's order as narrowly as possible. Thus, it directed that the networks give "equal time" to Congresswoman Chisholm, who was covered by the order, but not to Mayor Yorty. Compare, *Hon. Shirley Chisholm*, 35 F.C.C. 2d 579 (1972) and *Hon. Sam Yorty*, 35 F.C.C. 2d 570 (1972).

35. *The Goodwill Station, Inc.*, 40 F.C.C. 362 (1962).

36. *Robert L. Wyckoff*, 40 F.C.C. 370 (1962).

37. *Aspen Institute Program on Communications and Society*, 55 F.C.C. 2d 697, 700 (1975).

38. Ibid.

39. The condition that the event be broadcast live later was relaxed somewhat to allow delayed broadcasts of debates as much as 24 hours after the event without incurring "equal time" obligations. *Delaware Broadcasting Co.*, 60 F.C.C. 2d 1030, *aff'd sub. nom. Office of Communication v. FCC*, No. 76–1878 (D.C. Cir. September 11, 1978).

40. Roscoe L. Barrow, "The Presidential Debates of 1976: Toward a Two Party Political System," 46, *Cincinnati L. Rev.*, 123 (1977).

41. This charge focused particularly on the fact that in the *Aspen* decision the FCC also held that broadcasts of a candidate's press conferences were exempt from the "equal time" requirement as coverage of "bona fide news events." Since press conferences of the incumbent Republican president were more likely to receive television coverage than were press conferences of the challenger, this decision was criticized as improperly favoring the incumbent.

42. *Chisholm v. FCC*, 538 F.2d 349 (D.C. Cir. 1975), *cert. denied*, 419 U.S. 1023 (1976). A later FCC decision that the broadcast of a taped recording of a debate the day after the actual event would still be "on-the-spot coverage of bona fide news events" and exempt from "equal time" (*Delaware Broadcasting Co.*, 60 F.C.C. 2d 1030 (1976)) also was upheld by a reviewing court. *Office of Communication v. FCC*, No. 76–1878 (D.C. Cir. September 11, 1978). That case had the effect of reaffirming the FCC decision that debates were exempt from equal time; the court held "[t]he range of interpretations of the on-the-spot coverage provision—amply illustrated by the FCC's shifting view of it—reflects the tension within the statute. Although that range is not unlimited, we cannot find that the Commission has exceeded its delegated authority " (Slip op. at 14–15).

43. The genesis of the Forums project and the presidential debates of 1976 which followed is described by their originators in Charles Benton and Gene Pokorny, "Prelude—Presidental Forums" (unpublished manuscript).

44. The Ford "slip" in the second debate and its ramifications are analyzed in Witcover, *Marathon: The Pursuit of the Presidency, 1972–1976*, pp. 597–608.

45. Press conference, October 14, 1976 (Washington, D.C.).

46. Jonathan Moore and Janet Fraser, eds., *Campaign for President* (Cambridge: Ballinger Publishing Co., 1977).

47. Stepehen Lesher with Patrick Caddell and Gerald Rafshoon, "Did the Debates Help Jimmy Carter?" (Paper prepared for the American Enterprise Institute Conference on the Future of Presidential Debates, Washington, D.C., October 1977), p. 2.

Chapter III

1. Edwin Emery, "Changing Role of the Mass Media in American Politics," *Annals of the American Academy of Political and Social Sciences*, Vol. 427 (September 1976), pp. 91–92.

2. Bernard R. Berelson, Paul F. Lazarsfeld, and William N. McPhee, "Political Processes: The Role of the Mass Media," in *The Process and Effects of Mass Communications*, rev. ed., eds. Wilbur Schramm and Donald F. Roberts (Urbana: University of Illinois Press, 1971), p. 656.

3. Steven H. Chaffe and Jack Dennis, "Presidential Debates: An Empirical Assessment" (Paper prepared for the American Enterprise Institute Conference on the Future of Presidential Debates, Washington, D.C., October 1977), p. 10.

4. David O. Sears, "The Debates in Light of Research: An Overview of the Effects"

(Paper presented to the American Political Science Association, Washington, D.C., September 1977), p. 66.

5. Sanders, "The Great Debates," pp. 21–22.

6. Kirkpatrick, "Presidential Candidate Debates: What Can We Learn from 1960?" p. 29.

7. Ibid.

8. Stanton, "A CBS View," p. 68.

9. Richard S. Salant, "The Televised Debates: A Revolution That Deserves a Future," *Public Opinion Quarterly*, Vol. 26, No. 3 (Fall 1962), p. 338.

10. White, *The Making of the President 1960*, p. 293.

11. *Newsweek*, November 8, 1976, p. 20.

12. Ibid.

13. James Karayn, "Presidential Debates—A Plan for the Future" (Paper prepared for the American Enterprise Institute Conference on the Future of Presidential Debates, Washington, D.C., October 1977; later retitled "The Case for Permanent Presidential Debates"), p. 13.

14. Richard B. Cheney, "The 1976 Presidential Debates: A Republican Perspective" (Paper prepared for the American Enterprise Institute Conference on the Future of Presidential Debates, Washington, D.C., October 1977), p. 41.

15. Chaffee and Dennis, "Presidential Debates: An Empirical Assessment," p. 6.

16. Herbert J. Gans, "Lessons 1976 Can Offer 1980," *Columbia Journalism Review*, Vol. 15 (January 1977), p. 28.

17. Stanton, "A CBS View," p. 68.

18. Sanders, "The Great Debates," p.14.

19. Chaffee and Dennis, "Presidential Debates: An Empirical Assessment," pp. 10–11.

20. Kirkpatrick, "Presidential Candidate Debates: What Can We Learn From 1960?" p. 29.

21. Moore and Fraser, eds., *Campaign for President*, p. 6.

22. Kirkpatrick, "Presidential Candidate Debates: What Can We Learn From 1960?" p. 18.

23. Katz and Feldman, "The Debates in the Light of Research," p. 190.

24. Ibid.

25. Robert MacNeil, *The People Machine* (New York: Harper & Row, 1968), p. 168.

26. Kirkpatrick, "Presidential Candidate Debates: What Can We Learn From 1960?" p. 18; MacNeil, *The People Machine*, p. 170; Sanders, "The Great Debates," p. 14.

27. MacNeil, *The People Machine*, p. 170.

28. Moore and Fraser, eds., *Campaign for President*, p. 142. According to pollster Robert Teeter, on the day of the debate Ford had an 11 percentage point lead over Carter, but one night later Carter had taken a 45 percentage point lead. James David Barber, "Characters in the Campaign: The Educational Challenge," in *Race for the Presidency*, ed., James David Barber (Englewood Cliffs, N.J.: Prentice-Hall, 1979), p. 127.

29. Kirkpatrick, "Presidential Candidate Debates: What Can We Learn From 1960?," p. 51.

30. American Political Science Association, "Report of the Commission on Presidential Campaign Debates" (Washington, D.C., 1964), p. 2.

31. *Newsweek*, September 27, 1976, p. 27.

32. Kirkpatrick, "Presidential Candidate Debates: What Can We Learn From 1960?" p. 29; *The Mass Media and Politics*, p. 393.

33. Lesher, "Did the Debates Help Jimmy Carter?" p. 3.

34. Salant, "The Television Debates: A Revolution That Deserves a Future," p. 342.

35. *Saturday Review*, November 13, 1976, p. 4.

36. Institute of Social Research, University of Michigan, "ISR Newsletter," Vol. 6, No. 1 (1978), p. 5.

37. Chaffee and Dennis, "Presidential Debates: An Empirical Assessment," pp. 11–12.

38. Cheney, "The 1976 Presidential Debates: A Republican Perspective," p. 36.

39. "ISR Newsletter," p. 5.

40. Katz and Feldman, "The Debates in the Light of Research," p. 190; Kirkpatrick, "Presidential Candidate Debates: What Can We Learn From 1960?" p. 29.

41. Chaffee and Dennis, "Presidential Debates: An Empirical Assessment," p. 14.

42. Thomas E. Patterson and Robert D. McClure, *The Unseeing Eye* (New York: G. P. Putnam's Sons, 1976). According to this study, during the 1972 presidential campaign (September 18, 1972–November 6, 1972) the network news broadcasts of ABC, CBS, and NBC devoted only 35 minutes, 46 minutes, and 26 minutes, respectively, to "key issues of the campaign," and only 20 minutes, 16 minutes, and 8 minutes, respectively, to "the candidates' key personal and leadership qualifications for office."

43. *Wall Street Journal*, June 8, 1976.

44. Salant, "The Television Debates: A Revolution That Deserves a Future," p. 339.

45. Emery, "Changing Role of the Mass Media in American Politics," p. 89; Paul R. Hagner and John Orman, "A Panel Study of the Impact of the First 1976 Presidential Debate" (Paper presented at the Annual Meeting of the American Political Science Association, Washington, D.C., September 1977).

46. Emery, "Changing Role of the Mass Media in American Politics," p. 89; Sears, "The Debates in the Light of Research: An Overview of the Effects," pp. 25–26, 56.

47. Hagner and Orman, "A Panel Study of the Impact of the First 1976 Presidential Debate," p. 8.

48. Salant, "The Television Debates: A Revolution that Deserves a Future," pp. 339–341.

49. Berelson, Lazarsfeld, and McPhee, "Political Processes: The Role of the Mass Media," p. 673.

50. Emery, "Changing Role of the Mass Media in American Politics," p. 91.

51. Hagner and Orman, "A Panel Study of the Impact of the First 1976 Presidential Debate," p. 6.

52. *Newsweek*, September 27, 1976, p. 35.

53. Samuel Lubell, "Personalities vs. Issues," in *The Great Debates*, ed. Sidney Kraus (Bloomington: University of Indiana Press, 1962), p. 160.

54. Katz and Feldman, "The Debates in the Light of Research," p. 190.

55. Kurt Lang and Gladys Engel Lang, *Politics and Television* (Chicago: Quadrangle Books, 1968), pp. 223–224.

56. Gans, "Lessons 1976 Can Offer 1980," p. 28.

57. Lesher, "Did the Debates Help Jimmy Carter?" pp. 8, 17.

58. Sears, "The Debates in the Light of Research: An Overview of the Effects," p. 63.

59. The impact of the 1976 debates on voting choices is unclear and the data "somewhat ambiguous." Gans, "Lessons 1976 Can Offer 1980," p. 28. Gans reports that in a CBS election day poll, 10 percent of the respondents indicated they had voted for a candidate because they were impressed with him in the debates; 12 percent reported having made up their minds about their choice during the debates. On the other hand, in an NBC election day poll about one-third of the respondents said they had made their choices on the basis of the debates. Sears found that "the debates only rarely were perceived as decisive in determining voting intentions according to voters' own self-reports, though they often were seen as influential. . . . But there is surprisingly little direct evidence on the impact of the debates on voter intentions." Sears, "The Debates in the Light of Research: An Overview of the Effects," p. 36. See also, Kirkpatrick, "Presidential Candidate Debates: What Can We Learn From 1960?" p. 28.

60. See generally, Sears, "The Debates in the Light of Research: An Overview of the Effects."

61. Chaffee and Dennis, "Presidential Debates: An Empirical Assessment," pp. 11–12.

62. Hagner and Orman, "A Panel Study of the Impact of the First 1976 Presidential Debate," pp. 5–7.

63. Lang and Lang, *Politics and Television*, p. 219.

Chapter IV

1. Michael Duval, Memorandum prepared for the Task Force on Televised Presidential Debates (October 9, 1978).

2. *En Banc Programming Inquiry*, 20 P&F Radio Reg. 1902 (1960). In 1972, Congress amended the Communications Act to add the specific requirement that broadcasters allow "reasonable access" to their stations for legally qualified candidates for federal elective office. Pub. L. 92–225, 86 Stat. 4; 47 U.S.C. §312(a)(7).

3. Waiver of Equal Time Law and the 1976 Presidential Debates: Hearing Before the Senate Committee on Commerce, 94th Cong., 2d Sess. (1976).

4. Richard S. Salant, "The Good But Not Great Non-Debates—Some Personal Notes" (1978) (unpublished manuscript), p. 22.

5. *Broadcasting*, October 25, 1976, p. 26.

6. Ibid., January 3, 1977, p. 62.

7. Ibid.

8. Ibid., December 4, 1978, p. 49.

9. In Stephen E. Gottleib, "The Role of Law in the Broadcast of Political Debate," 37 *Fed. Bar. J.* 1 (1978), the author argues that since it is the function of the press, including television news, to lead rather than respond to public opinion, it would be inappropriate for the networks to have responsibility for an event which should be responsive to majoritarian desires. The author also suggests that the networks are politicized to the same extent as newspapers, which traditionally support particular candidates, and should not have responsibility for the debates for this reason also.

10. *Broadcasting*, September 27, 1976, p. 106.

11. Walter R. Mears, "A View From the Inside," *Columbia Journalism Review*, Vol. 15 (January 1977), p. 24.

12. Elizabeth Drew, *American Journal: The Events of 1976* (New York: Random House, 1977), p. 439.

13. *Broadcasting*, October 4, 1976, p. 28.

14. Ibid., September 27, 1976, p. 25.

15. Ibid., October 4, 1976, p. 28.

16. *American Independent Party*, 62 F.C.C. 2d 4 (1976); the FCC decision was affirmed by the United States Court of Appeals for the District of Columbia Circuit without opinion, *McCarthy v. FCC*, No. 76–1915 (D.C. Cir.).

17. *Legally Qualified Candidates*, 43 P & F Radio Reg. 2d 905 (1978). A person may make the required "substantial showing" by presenting evidence that he or she has engaged to a substantial degree in activities commonly associated with political campaigning. These activities normally would include making campaign speeches, distributing campaign literature, issuing press releases, maintaining a campaign committee, and establishing campaign headquarters. The FCC has indicated that not all of these activities necessarily are required in each case to make a "substantial showing" and that there may be other activities not referred to here which would satisfy this requirement.

18. Sanders, "The Great Debates," p. 4.

19. Salant, "The Good But Not Great Non-Debates—Some Random Personal Notes," p. 11.

20. Karayn, "Presidential Debates—A Plan for the Future," pp. 19–20.

21. *The Washington Star*, October 26, 1976.

22. 2 U.S.C. §437c.

23. Mears, "A View From the Inside," p. 22.

Chapter V

1. Herbert A. Seltz and Richard D. Yoakam, "Production Diary of the Debates," in *The Great Debates*, ed. Sidney Kraus (Bloomington: University of Indiana Press, 1962), p. 114.

2. Review of Section 315 of the Communications Act: Hearings Before the Subcommittee on Communications of the Senate Commerce Committee, 87th Cong., 1st Sess. 41 (1961); *Broadcasting*, September 20, 1976, p. 21.

3. Continued network donation of television time for the debates could run afoul of the Campaign Act prohibition of corporate campaign contributions. The network telecast of a presidential campaign debate using television time made available without charge could be considered such a contribution. The law does define "contribution" to exclude any media "news story," and since the FCC has held the debates to be "bona fide news events," their carriage might be excluded from the contribution restriction as a "news story." The FCC interpretation is not binding on the FEC, however, and, in any event, is premised upon the absence of network control over the proceedings. If the networks controlled the debates as they did in 1960, the debates would not meet the FCC's test for a "bona fide news event" and might no longer be a "news story." It may be necessary, therefore, to seek clarification of this question to ensure the ability of the networks to continue to make television time available.

4. The Twentieth Century Fund Commission on Campaign Costs in the Electronic Era, *Voters' Ti.* (New York: The Twentieth Century Fund, 1969).

5. Campaign Study Group, "Increasing Access to Television for Political Candidates" (Institute of Politics, Harvard University, July 20, 1978), pp. 8–9. See also George H. White, "A Study of Access to Television for Political Candidates," A Report to the Campaign Finance Study Group (Institute of Politics, Harvard University, May 1978).

6. 2 U.S.C. § 431 (e)(1)(A).

7. The questions arose in part from an inquiry to the FEC by *New York Times* reporter Warren Weaver. In testimony before the Federal Election Commission in September 1977, the president of the League charged that the FEC opinion on debate funding problems in 1976 was "issued hastily, with limited discussion, merely in response to an informal inquiry from a newspaper reporter." In Weaver's initial article on the subject, which appeared in the *Times* on August 24, 1976, he wrote, "So far, none of the parties involved—the League, the two political parties or the candidates' campaign committees—has asked [the FEC] for a ruling. But the Commission, realizing late last week that serious problems were involved, began to examine the area on its own authority."

8. FEC, Opinion of Counsel No. 1975–82 (November 21, 1975).

9. Presidential candidates qualifying for "matching money" in the 1976 primaries included Democrats Birch Bayh, Lloyd Bentsen, Jerry Brown, Jimmy Carter, Frank Church, Fred Harris, Henry Jackson, Ellen McCormack (running as an anti-abortion candidate), Terry Sanford, Milton Shapp, Sargent Shriver, and Morris Udall and Republicans Gerald Ford and Ronald Reagan. In May 1977, during an FEC audit, Milton Shapp was determined to have been ineligible for matching funds, and was required to return the funds paid him to the U.S. Treasury. No minor party or new party candidates qualified, although they had the theoretical ability to do so under the law.

10. *The Washington Star*, "Niggling Over the Debates," August 26, 1976, editorial page.

11. Letter from the League of Women Voters' Education Fund to the FEC, August 25, 1976.

12. FEC, Policy Statement on Presidential Debates, August 30, 1976.

13. Hearings on Candidate Debates, FEC, September 12, 1977.

14. *The Washington Post*, September 20, 1976.

15. Press Release, FEC, December 9, 1977.

16. 26 U.S.C. §501(c)(3).

17. *Buckley v. Valeo*, 24 U.S. 1, 9 –5 (1976).

Chapter VI

1. Mazo et al., "The Great Debates," p. 2.

2. Kirkpatrick, "Presidential Candidate Debates: What Can We Learn From 1960?" p. 11.

3. Professors Polsby and Wildavsky have concluded that "if one [candidate] is an incumbent, or feels himself securely in the lead, there is little incentive to debate." Nelson W. Polsby and Aaron Wildavsky, *Presidential Elections* (New York: Charles Scribner's, 1976), 4th ed., p. 179. After the 1960 debates, columnist John Crosby wrote: "Certainly no President . . . is willingly going to present his opponent with such a vast opportunity to undo him." Sanders, "The Great Debates," p. 24.

4. Quoted in *Nation*, September 11, 1976.

5. Sanders, "The Great Debates," p. 25.

6. MacNeil, *The People Machine*, p. 178.

7. Kirkpatrick, "Presidential Candidate Debates: What Can We Learn From 1960?" p. 9.

8. Ibid., p. 10.

9. Ibid., p. 8.

10. Ibid.

11. MacNeil, *The People Machine*, p. 173.

12. *The New Republic*, November 7, 1960.

13. American Political Science Association, "Report of the Commission on Presidential Campaign Debates," p. 2.

14. Kirkpatrick, "Presidential Candidate Debates: What Can We Learn From 1960?" p. 11.

15. *Broadcasting*, February 2, 1976, p. 33.

16. MacNeil, *The People Machine*, p. 176.

17. Ibid.

18. Rubin, *Political Television*, p. 44.

19. Sanders, "The Great Debates," p. 10, quoting *The Reporter*, November 10, 1960.

20. Rubin, *Political Television*, p. 45.

21. Polsby and Wildavsky, *Presidential Elections*, pp. 178–179; Mazo et al., "The Great Debates," pp. 2–3.

22. Cheney, "The 1976 Presidential Debates: A Republican Perspective," pp. 23, 27. Ford had received an earlier strategy memo from his staff suggesting that the debates should serve as the centerpiece for the entire Ford campaign:

> Given the constraints on time and spending, we cannot defeat Carter in a beauty contest. Therefore, we must steer the campaign back to the issues, even though the American public does not really care about them at a substantive level of detail.
>
> We can steer the campaign onto the issues and prove the President's desire and superior ability to be President by challenging Carter to a series of four debates in the month of October. One debate is risky and less likely to really focus on issues. Thus, the President can challenge Carter to debates on domestic affairs, the economy, national defense and foreign policy. In this situation, we can maximize the advantage of incumbency, since the President is far more knowledgeable, experienced and balanced than Carter. To be fair, we can make the challenge September 1 and offer any

briefings or information over the month that Carter would like to have. If he accepts, he acknowledges ignorance; if he declines, arrogance.

If he declines, the President can schedule four, fifteen minute unilateral policy speeches, thereby repackaging his policy positions and underscoring Carter's fuzziness.—Martin Schramm, *Running for President 1976* (New York: Stein and Day, 1977), p. 291.

23. *The Washington Post*, October 24, 1976.
24. Lesher, "Did the Debates Help Jimmy Carter?" p. 11.
25. Ibid. p. 4.
26. Mears, "A View From the Inside," p. 21.
27. *The Washington Post*, November 28, 1976, p. A7.
28. *Saturday Review*, November 13, 1976, p. 4.
29. *The Mass Media and Politics*, p. 445.
30. *Broadcasting*, January 3, 1977, p. 58.
31. Stanley Kelley, Jr., "Campaign Debates: Some Facts and Issues," *Public Opinion Quarterly* Vol. 26, No. 3 (Fall 1962), pp. 351–352.
32. Mazo et al., "The Great Debates," p. 10.
33. Karayn, "Presidential Debates—A Plan for the Future."
34. *West Virginia v. Barnette*, 319 U.S. 624 (1943); *Wooley v. Maryland*, 97 S. Ct. 1428 (1977).
35. *Buckley v. Valeo*, 24 U.S. 1, 15 (1976); *Monitor Patriot Co. v. Roy*, 401 U.S. 265, 272 (1971).
36. *Buckley v. Valeo*, 424 U.S. at 39, quoting *Williams v. Rhodes*, 393 U.S. 23, 32 (1968).
37. *Buckley v. Valeo*, 424 U.S. at 57.
38. *Civil Service Comm'n v. Letter Carriers*, 413 U.S. 548, 564 (1973); *Pickering v. Board of Education*, 391 U.S. 563 (1968) (restrictions on freedom of speech of public school teachers necessary to promote efficiency and effectiveness).

Chapter VII

1. Although more than 100 persons informed the Federal Election Commission that they were candidates for the presidency in 1976, fifteen persons appeared on the ballot in one or more states. Voters also had the choice of various write-in candidates, and in Nevada could cast a vote for "None of these candidates," a selection made by 5,108 voters.
2. *Lester Maddox*, 38 P&F Radio Reg. 2d 873 (1976); *Socialist Workers 1976 National Campaign Committee*, 67 F.C.C. 2d 182 (1976) (B'cast. Bur.), *aff'd*, FCC 76–875 (September 22, 1976); *American Independent Party*, 62 F.C.C. 2d (1976).
3. *Anderson v. Ford*, No. 76–1672 (D.D.C., September 17, 1976) (orders denying motions for preliminary injunction and summary judgment), *aff'd per curiam, McCarthy v. Carter*, No. 76–1865 (D.C. Cir., September 22, 1976), *cert. denied*, 429 U.S. 876 (1976). See also, *Socialist Workers Party v. U.S.*, No. 76–1897 (D.C. Cir. September 30, 1976) (*aff'g per curiam Socialist Workers Party*, FCC 76–875) *cert. denied*, 429 U.S. 890 (1976); *McCarthy v. FCC*, No. 76–1915 ((D.C. Cir.) (consolidated with *McCarthy v. Carter, supra*).
4. Wisconsin Socialist Workers Party Campaign Committee, FCC Mimeo 7641 (September 21, 1978).
5. "Third Parties: A Struggle for Attention," *Congressional Quarterly*, October 16, 1976, p. 2971.
6. In this century, minor party candidates have received 5 percent or more of the vote only four times and have received electoral votes only three times:

Candidate	Year	% of Vote	Electoral Vote	Party
Theodore Roosevelt	1912	27.4	88	Bull Moose
Eugene Debs	1912	6.0	—	Socialist
Robert LaFollette	1924	16.6	13	Progressive
George C. Wallace	1968	13.5	46	American Independent

7. "Third Parties: A Struggle for Attention," p. 2975.

8. Germond and Witcover, "Presidential Debates: An Overview," pp. 25–26.

9. Charles A. Seipman, "Were They 'Great'?" in *The Great Debates*, ed. Sidney Kraus, p. 140.

10. *Voters' Time*, p. 26.

11. Roscoe L. Barrow, "The Presidential Debates of 1976: Toward a Two Party Political System," 46 *Cincinnati L. Rev.*, (1977) 123, 134–135.

12. Sanders, "The Great Debates," p. 8.

13. Hearings on H.R. 8677 and H.R. 8628 Before the Subcomm. on Communications and Power of the House Comm. on Interstate and Foreign Commerce, 92nd Cong., 1st Sess., 162–64 (1971).

14. *Broadcasting*, March 14, 1977, p. 50.

15. Ibid., January 3, 1977, p. 60.

16. Barrow, "The Presidential Debates of 1976," p. 145. The six candidates meeting the 3 percent test were:

Candidate	Year	% of Vote	Party
Theodore Roosevelt	1912	27	Bull Moose
Eugene Debs	1912	6	Socialist
Allen Benson	1916	3	Socialist
Eugene Debs	1920	3	Socialist
Robert LaFollette	1924	16	Progressive
George Wallace	1968	13	American Independent

17. Various similar standards for determining significant candidates as a limitation on the "equal time" requirement have been suggested from time-to-time. For example, it has been proposed that major candidates be defined as candidates who are (1) the nominee of a political party whose presidential candidate polled at least 4 percent of the vote in the preceding presidential election, or (2) supported by petitions numbering at least 1 percent of that vote. Richard Salant, *Political Campaigns and the Broadcaster* (Cambridge: Harvard University Press, 1958), p. 360.

18. Under the Presidential Election Campaign Fund Act, 26 U.S.C. §9001, *et seq.*, which governs the entitlement of candidates to receive federal funds for their campaign, a person is to be considered a "candidate" in a presidential election if the person: (a) has been nominated by a "major party" *or* (b) "has qualified to have his name on the election ballot (or to have the names of electors pledged to him on the ballot) as the candidate of a political party . . . in ten or more States." 26 U.S.C. §9002(2).

The term "major party" is defined by the law as a political party whose candidate for the office of president in the preceding presidential election received 25 percent or more of the total popular vote cast for that office. 26 U.S.C. §9002(6). Thus, to be sufficiently "significant" to receive federal funding, a candidate must be the nominee of a party whose candidate for the presidency received 25 percent or more of the vote in the last election or, if representing a party which does not meet this test, must have qualified to have his or her name on the ballot in ten or more states.

The federal election law also distinguishes among those candidates who have qualified for some federal funding. Candidates of a "major party," as defined above, receive the greatest benefits. Candidates of a "minor party," defined as a party whose candidate for president in the preceding election received 5 percent or more but less than 25 percent of the total popular vote, and candidates of a "new party," defined as a party which does not meet the "minor party" standard, receive lesser benefits. The law makes no provision for independent candidates.

19. See Chapter IV, note 17.

20. Another distinction among candidates is made by the Secretary of the Treasury and an Advisory Committee on Protection of Presidential Candidates; they determine in each presidential election year which candidates should be provided with Secret Service protection. In the 1968 and 1972 elections, the Advisory Committee chose candidates based upon its subjective judgment as to the significance of the candidates. In 1976, the committee issued formal guidelines which provided that a candidate would be entitled to Secret Service protection if the candidate had qualified under the federal election laws to receive public funds in the primary election campaign (the test for federal funding in the primaries is that the candidate have received contributions totaling at least $5,000 in each of 20 states and composed of contributions of no more than $250 each). This plan proved unworkable, however, when several assassination plots against President Ford were uncovered in the fall of 1975, prior to the disbursement of federal funds to the candidates. Consequently, the Advisory Committee altered the standard to include any candidate who had collected $100,000 in campaign contributions after January 1, 1975. Using this test, candidates Bentsen, Carter, Jackson, Sanford, Udall, Wallace, Harris, Reagan, Shriver, and Ford received protection. Peter Camejo, the candidate of the Socialist Workers party, and independent candidate Eugene McCarthy requested protection at that time but were refused; McCarthy was given protection in September 1976 after qualifying for a place on numerous state ballots.

21. "Report of the Commission on Presidential Debates," p. 7.

22. *The New York Times*, August 31, 1976.

23. Seipman, "Were They 'Great'?" p. 1 0. Under present law, the appearance of a minor party or independent candidate in broadcast time made available in lieu of inclusion in a debate probably would require that "equal time" be accorded other candidates. Adoption of a system wherein major party candidates appear in debates and leading minor party or independent candidates received comparable time of their own would require, therefore, a revision of Section 315 to make the latter time exempt from "equal time."

24. Under the Barrow plan, any broadcast time given a "major party" candidate would require equal time for other "major party" candidates and one-half as much time for "minor party" candidates; any time given "minor party" candidates would require equal time for other "minor party" candidates and one-half as much time for major party" candidates; any time given to new party or independent candidates would not require that time be given to other candidates. Barrow, 46 *Cincinnati L. Rev.*, (1977) 123, 146.

25. Nixon believed that a three party debate with Humphrey and Wallace would have been clearly to his disadvantage:

> He [Humphrey] knows that he's running third in the new South. So he's trying to use Wallace to beat Nixon in the new South. He feels apparently that by having debates that maybe Wallace can win the whole perimeter of the South which I otherwise might win and I'm just not going to play that game.—*New York Times*, September 28, 1968, p. 1.

26. Letter of September 8, 1976, App. to Affidavit of Eugene McCarthy filed in *McCarthy v. Carter*, No. 76–1697 (D.C. Cir.).

Chapter VIII

1. The most thorough study of presidential debate formats appears to be the Political Campaign Debate Research Project of West Chester State College (West Chester, Pennsylvania) under the direction of Professor Myles Martel.

2. *The Washington Post*, November 28, 1976, p. A7.

3. Memo to Debate Steering Committee, League of Women Voters, 1976.

4. F. Clifton White, "Presidential Debate of 1976" (Remarks prepared for the Annual Meeting of the American Political Science Association, Washington, D.C., September 1977).

5. Nelson W. Polsby, "Debatable Thoughts on Presidential Debates" (Paper prepared for the American Enterprise Institute Conference on the Future of Presidential Debates, Washington, D.C., October 1977), p. 6.

6. J. Jeffery Auer, "The Counterfeit Debates," in *The Great Debates*, ed. Sidney Kraus, p. 146.

7. Myles Martel, "Presidential Debate Formats: A Resource Presentation for the Task Force on Presidential Debates of the Twentieth Century Fund," November 17, 1978, Appendix B.

8. Seltz and Yoakam, "Production Diary of the Debates," pp. 77–78.

9. *The Mass Media and Politics*, p. 396.

10. *Broadcasting*, August 23, 1976, p. 15.

11. *Economist*, October 2, 1976, p. 401. Professor Myles Martel points out that direct examination is only one, and not the most common, of the debate formats generally in use. Martel, "Presidential Debate Formats," p. 6.

12. Chaffee and Dennis, "Presidential Debates: An Empirical Assessment," p. 23.

13. Ibid.

14. Karayn, "Presidential Debates—A Plan for the Future," p. 15.

15. *The Washington Star*, October 26, 1976.

16. *Broadcasting*, January 3, 1977, p. 56.

17. Mazo et al., "The Great Debates," p. 216.

18. Polsby, "Debatable Thoughts on Presidential Debates," p. 6.

19. Daniel J. Boorstin, "From News-Gathering to News-Making: A Flood of Pseudo-Events," *The Process and Effects of Mass Communication*, eds. Schramm and Roberts, p. 148.

20. Polsby, "Debatable Thoughts on Presidential Debates," pp. 16–17.

21. Rubin, *Political Television*, p. 20.

22. Mears, "A View From the Inside," p. 23.

23. Robert W. Sarnoff, "An NBC View," in *The Great Debates*, ed. Sidney Kraus, p. 60.

24. "Report of the Commission on Presidential Campaign Debates," p. 27.

25. *The Washington Star*, October 26, 1976.

26. *The Mass Media and Politics*, pp. 37, 425.

27. Mickelson, *The Electric Mirror*, p. 211.

28. Ibid, p. 202.

29. Frank Stanton, "The Case for Political Debates on TV," *New York Times Magazine*, January 19, 1964, p. 69.

30. Katz and Feldman, "The Debates in the Light of Research," p. 218.

31. "Report of the Commission on Presidential Campaign Debates," p. 22.

32. Mears, "A View From the Inside," p. 22.

33. Mickelson, *The Electric Mirror*, p. 211.

34. Kirkpatrick, "Presidential Candidate Debates: What Can We Learn From 1960?" p. 22.

35. Karayn, "Presidential Debates: A Plan for the Future," p. 11.

36. Ibid., p. 14.

37. Kirkpatrick, "Presidential Candidate Debates: What We Can Learn From 1960?" p. 18.

38. *Newsweek*, September 27, 1976, p. 31.

39. Ibid.

40. Salant, "The Television Debates: A Revolution That Deserves a Future," p. 348.

41. Kirkpatrick, "Presidential Candidate Debates: What Can We Learn From 1960?" p. 25; "Report of the Commission on Presidential Campaign Debates," pp. 6–10.

42. Karayn, "Presidential Debates—A Plan for the Future," p. 15.

43. Gans, "Lessons 1976 Can Offer 1980," p. 28.

44. Mazo et al., "The Great Debates," p. 20.

45. Salant, "The Good But Not Great Non-Debates—Some Random Personal Notes," pp. 26–27.

46. *The New York Times*, October 24, 1976.